MARKETING FOR THE MAD (WO)MEN OF TOMORROW

'THE REAL FACT OF THE MATTER IS THAT NOBODY READS ADS.

PEOPLE READ WHAT INTERESTS THEM. SOMETIMES IT'S AN AD.'[1]

HOWARD GOSSAGE, ORIGINAL MAD MAN

WIM VERMEULEN

MARKETING FOR THE MAD WOMEN OF TOMORROW

STRONG BRANDS IN A WORLD OF ALGORITHMS

LANNOO
CAMPUS

This book was originally published as *Marketing voor de mad men van morgen*, LannooCampus Publishers (2018).

D/2018/45/331 – ISBN 978 94 014 5411 7 – NUR 802

Cover design: Gert Degrande | De Witlofcompagnie
Interior design: Fulya Toper
Translation: Hermine Van Coppenolle

© Wim Vermeulen & Lannoo Publishers nv, Tielt, 2018.

LannooCampus Publishers is a subsidiary of Lannoo Publishers, the book and multimedia division of Lannoo Publishers nv.

LannooCampus Publishers
Erasme Ruelensvest 179 box 101
3001 Leuven
Belgium
www.lannoocampus.com

CONTENT

A book about marketing and advertising without case studies is inconceivable. In this book, I therefore discuss about forty prime examples. Related pictures and videos are all available on the internet, but to make things easier, we have collected all visual aids on www.wimvermeulen.com

This icon indicates that material related to an example can be found on the website.

INTRODUCTION

'What happened to the funny ads?'[2], American business magazine *Fast Company* asked in September of 2017. Where have the big marketing campaigns gone, those that could move people to tears? Those that launched and sold out products, those that saved companies from bankruptcy overnight?

We are under the impression that those no longer exist. Why would they? The world has changed too much, just like the consumer and the media. So why would we still annoy consumers with mass media advertisements? Would it not be much more cost-effective to contact them directly? Thanks to the right data, we are able to convey our message when it matters most, right before an online purchase for example. We can measure and direct the effect on the spot. Then why, for heaven's sake, still bother with big campaigns? They cost tons of money and reach tons of consumers that do not even have to be reached. On top of that, the campaign's effect is not immediately or directly noticeable and more difficult to translate into spreadsheets. Hasn't it become silly to even try?!

That is what we, marketeers, were told for years. It has seeped into what we think and what we do. It is the starting point of our briefings and lays the foundation of the campaigns we bring to the consumer. However, it is a wrong point of view entirely. A steadily growing mountain of data shows that the effectiveness of our campaigns has been declining. Our work is weakening brands and is negatively influencing sales. That can never be the point, quite the opposite: we have to stop this trend. Sooner rather than later. After all, an industry making a product with a negative ROI is doomed to disappear.

We assume too easily that the decreasing effectiveness of our campaigns has to do with 'the change'. We have to stop feeling sorry for ourselves and stop blaming it all on the digital revolution. Nor is it the millennials being sick of any form of advertising or the decreasing popularity of traditional media. The causes behind the decreasing efficacy of our campaigns are entirely our own.

WE DO NOT CEASE TO CONFUSE OURSELVES

Next time Google pops up on your screen, type in 'The death of the TV-commercial'. You will be stunned by what you read. The commercial is dead. Or not. Or maybe a little. In 2017 we came to the conclusion that the TV-commercial is not dead at all, on the contrary: it is the foundation of the most effective campaigns. This assessment ends a debate that, according to Google, started in 2011. Six years of confusion summarized on one Google page. Type in 'The death of the banner ad' and you will see it again. We have declared almost all advertising techniques and media dead. We seem to be having the uncontrollable urge to kill off something old every time something new comes along. How does this make us feel? Confused, and being confused in times of great change is just not a good idea. We have to rid ourselves of this feeling however, because the changes will keep coming. In chapter one we will discuss the speed of these changes, while in chapter two we will focus on the resulting confusion.

WE ARE NOT FOLLOWING THE GROUND RULES

Every discipline has its ground rules. An architect wanting to build a skyscraper has to adhere to the laws of physics. He or she can choose whether or not to follow the latest design trends, but simply cannot ignore the basic laws of physics. Marketeers are architects as well, but we have been building skyscrapers without paying much attention to the laws of physics, which is why our towers are threatening to collapse, one by one.

Our 'laws of physics' were written by advertising giants like Bill Bernbach and David Ogilvy. Bernbach stands for the B in DDB, the famous international advertising agency. He wrote a memo in 1947 that launched the creative advertising revolution in the 1950s and he led by example, creating many of the now classics in advertising. David Ogilvy founded Ogilvy & Mather, today a part of WPP, the world leader in advertising. He was the other revolutionary. Together they reinvented our field. If these men could see our work today, however, they would show us the door. We have been and still are blatantly breaking their laws. It is time we reinstate their legacy. In chapter three we will discuss each of these giants of advertising, making it easier to understand what they can teach us.

It all started with the financial crisis of 2008. Companies were fighting to survive. All attention went to putting a halt to declining sales. We switched to short-term mode. However, even though the financial crisis has more or less been dealt with and even though it has been a decade now, we are still stuck in the same mind-set.

We are saturating the consumer with rational arguments. Promotions, competitions, discounts: everything that will pay off tomorrow we put into our action plans. Is it surprising then that the loyal customer has become a dying breed? That our consumers will jump from one promotion to the next without paying any attention to the brand? That the majority cannot even be bothered about the actual existence of brands? Of course not, right? Then why do we still continue to think only short-term?

Because we are stuck in a vicious cycle. Sales activation does exactly what it says on the tin: it activates sales. Stop the action and sales will drop again. We use them to create peaks, but we are not achieving sustainable growth. This is attainable only by combining sales activities with brand building. We even know the most efficient budgetary mix: 60% of our yearly advertising budget has to go to brand building, 40% to short-term sales activation. However, we are not adhering to this ratio. We are only thinking short-term and we are launching one sales activation after the other. But that only heightens our consumer's sensitivity to promotions. This dooms us to keep having to activate sales. We will discuss this vicious cycle in-depth in chapter four.

THE ALGORITHMS ARE AT THE DOOR

Amazon Echo's success is spectacular. Its sales in the first year after launch rival those of the iPhone. Not too shabby for a brand new product. No wonder so many similar products are being launched. Google, Microsoft, Apple, Sony: they all want their share.

Amazon Echo is a plastic cube, a smart speaker, that houses Alexa. Alexa is a personal assistant, like Siri or Cortana. An algorithm. What Alexa does very well is help you shop. When, for example, we are out of butter, we can simply say: 'Alexa, we need butter'. Alexa jots it down on our virtual grocery list. If we do not want to buy anything else, we just ask Alexa to put in our order. The system does so immediately. Piece of cake.

Think about a non-virtual grocery list. What does it say? Milk, butter, water, cheese, fruit, laundry detergent or yogurt, right? We usually describe products generically. Only occasionally do we add a brand to the mix. That is what we do when we call on Alexa. 'Alexa, order water.' 'Alexa, buy two tubs of ice cream.' We keep it general; it is up to Alexa to complete the order and fill in the brand. The algorithm decides based on pricing, scores, reviews and other rational factors.

However, do we want to leave the decision making to Alexa? Is it not in our best interest that the consumer is consciously asking for our brands? Yes, but only strong brands will be able to pull that off, because only strong brands that rate high in brand preference get called by their names. For example: 'Alexa, buy two tubs of Ben & Jerry's.' If your brand is not strong, that needs to change. Fast, because Alexa or Siri are obviously not coming alone. There is an invasion of algorithms going on, as we will discuss in chapter five.

HOW DO WE MAKE BRANDS STRONG, FAST?

To answer this question, we will dive into the work of a number of neuroscientists. It is baffling how much progress is made in the field of neuropsychology. The consumer's brain says more about their behavior than they possibly could themselves. We also understand better and better how the consumer makes decisions and what role advertising plays in this process.

A dive into data is indispensable as well, based on analyses by the IPA database (Institute of Practitioners in Advertising). At the moment it is the biggest advertising database in the world, counting more than 1200 case studies starting from 1998. Of course, we have to mention the classics, but we will also look at some of the work by twenty-first century brands, as well as examine the research on more than 2,200 campaigns sent in for the Effectiveness Awards of the IPA.

We will take a detailed look at forty of the most effective campaigns. They made brands stronger and blew up sales, paving the way for an impressive increase in results. They also succeeded in making the consumer discuss and share the campaign, which more often than not the consumer did loudly and convincingly, thus creating extra share of voice and multiplying the original investments by the brand.

What do these campaigns teach us? All forty of them have a number of common characteristics, which we will uncover and compare to subsequently use them in the construction of a new model. This new model can stand up to the challenges of advertising in the twenty-first century. We have called it the 'TapForward Communication Model' and, currently, it is the most fitting model to promote brands in today's digital world. It outperforms the existing communication models on both brand building and increasing sales. We will discuss this new model in chapter five as well.

TO THE MAD (WO)MEN OF TOMORROW

Advertising is a craft. Our craft is to seduce. We seduce consumers to pick one brand over another. David Ogilvy said it loud and clear: 'Your role is to sell, do not let anything distract you from the sole purpose of advertising.'[3]

The giants of advertising revolutionized our field in the '60s. Advertising had evolved into a game of numbers and strict laws which crippled results. People like Bill Bernbach thought this needed to be done differently. This is what his memo was about. The document went down in history as the start of a creative revolution. We know what it brought us: a new golden age for our industry.

Today we are in a similar situation. It has all become a bit too technical. Our thinking has been confined to the short-term. We are forgetting our laws of physics and we are not ceasing to confuse ourselves. It is time to take back control. It is time for a new memo. It is time to baffle our consumers again, instead of being a nuisance. Time to make brand-strengthening campaigns that succeed in driving sales through the roof.

It is time.

It is your time.

CHAPTER 1

THE WORLD IS RUNNING ON A NEW OPERATING SYSTEM

'I FEAR THE DAY THAT TECHNOLOGY
WILL SURPASS OUR HUMAN INTERACTION.'

ALBERT EINSTEIN

The advertisements we produce are usually not all that great. The banners even less so, never mind those promoted posts on Facebook. Every once in a while, though, we still manage to get it right. Then we can see the true magic of what we do. Suddenly, a simple idea changes the whole perception of a company or makes a product successful as if from thin air. This is the real work. When this happens, it is utter bliss. Unfortunately, it does not happen very often.

In 2006, Dove published a video on the internet. It is a little over a minute long and shows a model walking into a studio. The model is first shown in all her natural beauty and imperfections. Human imperfections. For a second we get the feeling this beauty is attainable. That we do not look too bad ourselves. Next, the model gets her hair and make-up done. The flaws are fading away, transforming the model into a vision we know all too well: one of unattainable beauty. She gets her pictures taken, which are then photo-shopped. The neck becomes longer, the eyes a bit bigger, every imperfection of the skin gets brushed away, the face becomes completely perfect. Unattainably perfect. Why did Dove want to expose this? The answer follows quickly: 'No wonder our perception of beauty is distorted. Take part in the Dove Real Beauty Workshops.' This clip was viewed around the world and went down in history as the first viral ad.

Dove did something very brave: the brand took a stance. It sided with women and condemned society's beauty standards. It tried to break a taboo. Bold, given the film came out at a time when runway models had to be skinny. Being skinny is a beauty ideal so forceful it can take lives: model Ana Carolina Reston Macan died of anorexia in 2006. It was in that same year and against that same backdrop that Dove decided to go against the flow and challenge the norm. For a brand that ultimately needs to increase its sales, this was a huge gamble. Dove knew it would most likely gain new clients, clients supporting the cause, but the brand could not have been sure how many consumers it would lose.

However, the campaign effectively broke the taboo. In 2004 only 23% of women felt that they influenced the general definition of beauty. Ten years later their share had gone up to almost 70%, partially thanks to Dove and its powerful idea.

We, as marketeers, only manage to achieve such a thing every once in a while. It is extremely difficult. You have to be able to sense what your consumer is thinking. You also have to be aware of what you can or cannot do as a brand. You need to have a vision and fully commit to it. Especially in a time where most companies focus on short-term results, this is no easy feat.

CHANGE MAKES US STRONGER

The transformational phase we find ourselves in today only renders matters even more difficult. It seems our trade is up in the air. Our business model is in freefall. The types of creative ideas that have been the cornerstones of all successful campaigns for years, have lost their edge, or so we believe. Consumers use ad blockers or delay watching television shows, only to avoid seeing our work. To add insult to injury, all of this is happening at the same time.

There are two ways to go about this. Either we can scream: 'Help! This will not end well. The advertising industry is doomed, the next victim of the digital disruption!' or we can keep our cool and look at this evolution as the next in line of the many changes in our industry over the years. There have already been a few, and every time we have come out stronger.

In this book, we obviously prefer the second reaction. We are standing at the beginning of the next golden age of the advertising industry. Up until the beginning of the century, we understood the (simpler) set of rules and knew how to manipulate them. Then the world turned digital and we applied our analogue set of rules to it. Which of course did not work, the malaise in our business serves as a perfect *corpus delicti*. Two decades later, we (have started to) understand that it is no longer about digital or traditional marketing. It is about marketing in a digital world. A digital world running on a new operating system, an OS with its own set of rules. We are also realising that this is merely a brief moment in advertising history. With artificial intelligence pushing us to the verge of yet another acceleration, this current obstacle shall soon pale in comparison.

OFF TO A BOTH OLD AND NEW MODEL

We are under the impression that the original Mad (Wo)Men Model has been becoming less effective over the years. Players in digital media are shouting from the rooftops that traditional forms of advertisement are not cutting it

anymore, making us think that the whole of advertising is reducible to the efficient and inexpensive delivery of targeted messages. For them this is the age
of 'left-sided brain marketing'. A headline can only use twenty-five charac-
ters, the body copy merely ninety. This canvas forces us to fall back on a short,
rational rhetoric. Even though there are libraries filled with books pointing
out the importance of emotional arguments. This confuses us. We are given
the impression we need to choose between the old and the new. We do not!

As mentioned before, an architect building a skyscraper needs to adhere to
the laws of physics. He does not have a choice. It is advised that this same
architect also pays attention to the most current trends in design, but the
existence of the skyscraper does not depend on implementing these trends.
We do not have to choose between old and new at all. We have to keep what
works from the old and replace what does not with the new. This will put our
industry back on track. However, in order to do so, we will first have to understand where this track will lead us.

That is why we will first spend some time talking about the technological
changes. Because today, there is only one real certainty: change will keep
on coming, at a rapidly increasing pace. This makes today a very interesting
time, a time made for the innovative Mad (Wo)Men, ready and wanting to
move forward. Mad (Wo)Men who are not afraid to ride the (without a doubt,
turbulent) winds of change.

A NEW OPERATING SYSTEM

In December 2016, Amazon launched its 'no checkout' supermarket: Amazon
Go. A customer walks in, takes what he needs and walks back out. No more
wasting time stood in line at the counter, because there simply is none. A
combination of sensors, cameras, machines and mobile payments makes the
fully automated process possible. However, that is not the only thing Amazon
had in store that year: on the 7th of December 2016 they delivered a package by
drone. The package contained a bag of popcorn and a streaming device. The
time between the order and delivery was only thirteen minutes.

At the same time Uber launched its first fleet of autonomous taxis in Pitts-
burgh. In July 2017, the first batch of taxi drones performed a test flight in
Dubai. It is now possible for clients to simply step into a drone, type in his or
her destination after which it flies off, carrying the passenger along. Piaggio,
the company best known for their iconic Vespas, is experimenting with Gita,

an autonomous four-wheeled robot with a big 'stomach'. Customers can fill it up with whatever they like: groceries, backpacks, suitcases, whatever tickles their fancy. They can then just start walking and the robot will follow them anywhere they go.

Today, humanoid robots can be found in countless hospitals, helping patients on their roads to recovery, as well as in certain hotels, welcoming guests. Safe to say, the possibilities are endless and even though this is all 'digital', it still feels like a leap from the digital we know today: websites, mobile apps, social media and search engine marketing.

'Search' illustrates this perfectly. In 1996, Yahoo! was the biggest search engine. The company had staff categorising all of the websites they could find. There were only about 100,000 of them.[4] So in comparison to today, where we have access to more than 1.8 billion[5] websites, those in the Yahoo! database were merely a handful. The Yahoos, as Yahoo employees were called, were looking at the content of the sites to then put them into a category. Users could click on a category and have access to the list of websites, ready to start scrolling.

That was twenty years ago. Today we ask Siri, Alexa or Google assistant. A male or female voice (personal preference) answers. And we can ask any-thing. 'How tall is Mount Everest?' 'Find a hotel in Madeira.' 'Remind me to go to Tesco at 17:30.' 'How is traffic to work this morning?' 'How did I sleep last night?' 'Is it going to rain today? Send a text to my wife that I will be home on time.' Whatever we can think of, we can ask. This is how we are taking 'search' to the next level. Instead of typing in words or questions into a website, we are now referring to a virtual assistant. This requires less time and effort. And the consumer is greedy for more. Voice search is rising: 20% of all Google searches are voice activated. If you ask people when they started using it, 60% say 'less than twelve months ago'.[6] Things are changing fast.

The world of marketing is switching gears as well. Coca-Cola is looking into using Artificial Intelligence (AI) to make TV commercials that would score better than those made by traditional creative teams.[7] The experiment is part of their digital transformation plan. Mariano Bosaz, the Global Senior Digital Director at the company sees multiple uses for AI: scriptwriting, composing music, posting social media and buying media space.

Coca-Cola is not the only company looking into automating creative work. Jukedeck is a company that makes jingles and soundtracks, without musicians.[8] Computers handle the composing all by themselves. Hundreds of pages of sheet music are fed into their neural networks. The system learns how chords are built, what chords tend to follow each other and what the probability is of that happening. Two years ago, the result sounded like the music from an '80s videogame, today it sounds like the real deal.

It is clear that marketing is standing at a crossroads. Websites, apps and social media look like primitive tools from another era. In fact, they are. They were a part of the first digital era. Today we are entering the post digital age. That is what 'The world is running on a new operating system' entails.

THE LAW OF THE ACCELERATING RETURNS

It seems technological change is on steroids: it will not stop and it is rapidly gaining speed. Numerous times we wonder whether this is just a feeling or if it is actually the case. Well, it actually is. Two laws describe this speed of change. The first concerns modern history and modern history's acceleration: the Law of Accelerating Returns. The second is Moore's law.

Let us start with modern history and its accompanying acceleration. Regardless of the digital forces, there is a fundamental law in the history of humanity stating that changes will follow one another faster and faster, making the period between two changes shorter and shorter. Ray Kurzweil, a futurist, inventor and senior executive at Google, calls this the 'Law of Accelerating Returns'.[9] More developed societies develop themselves faster than less developed societies, because they are, simply, more developed to do so.

Tim Urban illustrates this quite astonishingly on his website 'Wait but Why'.[10] Urban wonders what would happen if we went back in time to 1750. We know we would find ourselves in a different world. Most of the people were living off of agriculture in the countryside. Houses were lit by candles. Pigeons took care of long range communications. Men wore wigs. Horses were the main means of transportation.

So, there we are, teleported to 1750. We stroll around for a while and enter a tavern. We meet some people. We invite one of them, a man, to join us in our travels back to 2018. We cannot imagine what that would do to a man from the 18th century. He sees incredibly wide lanes, with shiny capsules zooming past at immense speeds. We explain that this is our version of his carriages. He sees a window, not in a wall, but on a table. It is emitting light. A woman in the window looks at him. She asks him how he is doing. We explain that this woman is real and that she lives on the other side of the world. Magic! Witchcraft! We show him a small, rectangular box. He sees a map with a pulsing blue dot. We explain that the dot shows where he is. We zoom in. The map disappears and the street he sees in front of him appears on the box. The street is in the box. Sorcery. Pure wizardry. We do not have words to express what that man from the 18th century might feel at that time.

Imagine if that man wanted to share his experience with someone else, imagine him teleporting a woman from 1500 into 1750. That woman would not have the same unthinkable, mind-blowing experience, because life in the year 1500 did not differ enough from that in 1750. Even the ancient Greeks would probably not have been equally flabbergasted if they woke up in 1750. The man would have to go all the way back to the beginning of the agrarian revolution about 13,000 years ago to cause the same kind of shock.

This is what Kurzweil calls the 'Law of Accelerating Returns', and it is still applicable today. Changes between 1985 and 2015 were way bigger than during the thirty years between 1955 and 1985. You have to wonder where this might end. Well, that depends on who you are asking. Ask Kurzweil and your answer is clear: never. Change is permanent. The progress experienced in the 20th century will be achieved, at the rate of the year 2000, in twenty years. He believes we have realized the equivalent of all the progress of the previous century between 2000 and 2014. And if he is right, then we will make that same progress about a thousand times in this century. In other words, if we were to step into a time machine to 2050, we would probably experience the same as the man from 1750 did. What a future we have to look forward to!

MOORE'S LAW

However, Kurzweil's law of accelerating returns is not the only theory behind the onslaught of technical innovation. There is also *Moore's law*.

Gordon Moore is one of the pioneers of Silicon Valley. In 1957 he co-founded Fairchild Semiconductor, a company that designs and produces transistors. This company would become a key operation within the computer industry. However, in 1968, Gordon Moore left and, together with some other clever people, started a company called Intel that would become known from their

'80s slogan 'Intel inside'. Intel was to become another one of the key companies in Silicon Valley. So, Moore is not just anyone, he is considered one of the most important thinkers and businessmen from the computer industry of the past fifty years.

In 1965, the American magazine *Electronics* celebrated its 35-year existence. For the April edition it asked Moore to predict the future of the chip industry for the next ten years. If anyone had an idea of what was to come, it was Moore, they thought. Moore wrote an article titled 'Cramming more components into integrated circuits'.[11] In it he described how the number of transistors per square inch on a chip was doubling each year. The number of transistors per chip determines the power of a computer. If that number doubled every year, then the power would as well. For him this was not a temporary phenomenon. He predicted that a doubling of computing power will take place every twelve to eighteen months.

It is difficult to comprehend what a doubling of the worldwide computing power at that pace actually means. Ever since the invention of the chip, the power of computers has, at a rough estimate, doubled twenty-seven times.[12] Let us say we compare this to a car driving 3 miles an hour. After doubling that twenty-seven times, it will be racing by at 416 million miles an hour. One more doubling and it would be over a billion miles per hour. At that speed, it would take five minutes to travel to Mars.

That is the scale we have to think of when we talk about the evolution in computing power. We are driving today at 416 miles per hour. Therefore, we should not be surprised that we suddenly have access to human-like robots, artificial intelligence, self-driving cars and voice operated assistants like Alexa and Siri.

It is true that Moore's law is slowing down. We are not doubling our computing power every eighteen months anymore. However, today we are on our way to the 28th doubling and our car is now driving at over a million mph. The hockey stick effect is now fully manifesting.

Bearing those two laws in mind, it seems to make more sense that we jumped from websites to self-driving cars, robots and implementations of artificial intelligence in such a short time span. Even more, that today is not the end, but just a speck on a bigger timeline. This is not the first digital era anymore. This is the post-digital era. This is a world using a new operating system. We will continually be amazed, experiencing wonder after wonder. It will of course require a great deal of intellectual flexibility to be able to follow the exponential jumps technology will make every time Moore's law and the law of 'accelerating returns' come together to bring us to the next milestone.

THERE IS NO CRYSTAL BALL

In 2004, Blockbuster is the biggest video rental company in the United States. It has fifty million clients, sixty thousand employees and more than nine thousand outlets in more than twelve countries. The revenues peak at 5.9 billion dollars, the company has a market value of five billion dollar. Blockbuster rules the video rental market.

In 2000, John Antioco, Blockbuster's CEO, receives a visit from Reed Hastings, CEO of Netflix.[13] Netflix at that point is an online DVD rental company. You pick the DVD you want on Netflix' website and the company sends you the disk by post. After watching, you just send it back. In comparison to renting a DVD at Blockbuster, the Netflix model had two considerable flaws: it is not instant (the DVD is sent by mail, at Blockbuster you just take it with you) and you can send the DVD back whenever you like. In other words: Netflix has no penalties for overdue DVDs. This, of course, is not a problem for the consumer, but it is for Antioco. These penalties, those fines, amount to a big part of the company's total revenue. As Netflix works with a subscription system, an income from fines is not a part of it.

Hastings meeting Antioco is like David meeting Goliath. A small challenger meeting the emperor, the ruler of the market. Hastings' proposal is simple, but bold: Blockbuster promotes Netflix in all its outlets. Netflix would, on its end, take care of Blockbuster online. For all of this, Blockbuster would get a 49% share of Netflix. However, Netflix is not even a blip on Antioco's radar. Hastings was lucky to even get an appointment. His offer sounds weak and unprofitable. Why would Antioco even consider making his clients wait a day or more for their DVDs? And more importantly, why would he ever give up fines? It is like slaying the goose with the golden eggs. Obviously, Hastings has no idea how the video rental business worked. He is kindly dismissed.

The rest, as they say, is history. In 2010, Blockbuster declared itself bankrupt. Today, Netflix is worth more than 150 billion dollars. Blockbuster completely misread the digitalization. It chose for the status quo, it chose to do nothing. That is why it was not prepared for the decline in revenue that was coming and, once it was there, there was no time left to innovate and find new revenue streams.

No one can predict the future, unfortunately. Ed Fries, one of the co-founders of gaming console Xbox, uses vintage postcards from twentieth century Europe to show us how our thinking about the future is limited by the knowledge we have today.[14] A century ago, we thought that we would be able, in 2012, to call each other with both sound and image. In other words: through something like Skype or Google Hangouts.

How people 100 years ago thought we'd be living today (Source: *Wired*)

The idea was visionary, but not too baffling. This was the age of the Lumière brothers and their cinematograph. Moving images were already being registered. Contemporary thinkers figured the combination of a projector and a land line would suffice to call through images. Of course they could not have known we would first need to invent the internet to make their vision come true. Their thinking was limited to what they knew back then.

At the beginning of the 20th century, there was already a lot of discussion about automatization. In the year 2000, we thought, it would not be the hairdresser cutting his clients' hair, a machine would. Automatization stood front and center in the future they had thought up for us back then. Not a single postcard contained anything that even resembles a computer. It makes sense as well. Nothing that existed in Victorian times even came close to a computer. We thought everything would be automated mechanically.

This shows that when we think about tomorrow, we are doing so within a contemporary framework. This holds us back from thinking about technology that does not come close to what we know today. And even if the technology or the bud of it exists, it is still difficult to imagine potential uses for it. Eventually, we manage, but it takes time. And the implementation that makes a technology or an invention mainstream is rarely the application the inventor had in mind.

Let us go back to Saturday the 28th of December 1895. In a backroom of the Grand Café in Paris the crowd is bustling in. The brothers Lumière will première their new machine: le cinématographe. With this machine, they would prove that they had succeeded in projecting movement that was true to life on a screen. The brothers have ten 'vues' ready for the crowd, 'Vues' is what they call their films. Every clip lasts about a minute. Their cinématographe can handle seventeen metres of film. No more.

A sense of curiosity and amazement hangs in the air. Images moving on a screen, no such thing has ever happened before. It would be a miracle if it worked. The lights go out. The cinématographe lights up. On a white canvas on the other side of the room an image becomes visible. First out of focus, but then increasingly clear. The crowd sees men and women exiting a factory. One after the other. It does not stop, and lasts for a minute and thirty seconds. Then the screen turns black. All is quiet. Suddenly the crowd jumps up and fills the room with oohs and aahs. Some people remain seated in their bewilderment, not entirely sure what just happened. The film is fittingly called 'La *sortie de l'usine Lumière à Lyon'*. Auguste and Louis Lumière are most known however for *'L'Arrivée d'un train à La Ciotat'*, a film they showed for the first time in January 1896. Legend has it that the crowd, when seeing the film, rushed to leave the room in bouts of panic. The image was so realistic that they thought the train would really drive into the room.

The brothers made hundreds of films. However, by 1900, they got bored of it all. It no longer was as exciting, those moving images. Stronger yet, Auguste declared cinema an invention without a future. They abandoned it all in order to focus on colour photography.

The brothers Lumières were not the only ones thinking that way. Some other filmmakers gave up too, but not D.W. Griffith. On the 8th of February 1915, his film *Birth of a Nation* appears. It is the story of two families during and after the American Civil War. The three-hour long silent film is announced as the 'most tremendous dramatic spectacle that the brain of man has yet produced'. It is a huge success. The filmmaker had found the application for the technology of the *cinématographe*: the feature film. Just like the brothers Lumière, Griffith was registering movement, but he was using it to tell a story. Today, *Birth of a Nation* is considered the mother of all films. Twenty years after the first screening by the Lumière brothers, the movie industry was born.

Promoting *Birth of a Nation* (Source: Reconciliation Services)

So, there is no crystal ball. This, of course, makes it more difficult to decide what the next steps for your brand should be. Our competitors cannot look into the future either though. The brands that remain, the brands that win, are those that are constantly innovating and trying new things. As such, they see where the next big thing might be, before their competitors do. Through trials, they reduce the learning curve faster. This allows them, once that big thing becomes mainstream, to profit from it. In a world running on a new operating system, any advantage you can get, could be a potential gold mine.

INNOVATING SOLIDITY

What does all this mean for the Mad (Wo)Men of tomorrow? More on this later, but for now it is already clear that the most important ability to have is *innovating solidity*. After all, you can look at the world of tomorrow in two different ways.

The first way is to assume that 'everything is under control'. No idea what might befall us in the future, but surely, it will be fine. The world, as of yet, has not succumbed to all the technological change. The second is more of an 'Oh shit' kind of mindset. The speed of the upcoming changes is entirely unprecedented, unlike anything we have seen. We are at the beginning of the AI revolution. Few people are able to say what this will bring, and some important people are calling out, louder and louder, that humanity is in danger. Others think we are taking the last step to human immortality. Oh, shit!

Depending on the side you choose, this either sounds completely terrifying, or extremely exciting. The Mad (Wo)Men of tomorrow find themselves in the second category. They adore innovation. They love the risk it brings, but also the feeling of satisfaction when innovation works out. However, they know that it all needs to work within a predefined strategy. Innovating to innovate is fun, but unbecoming. The Shiny Object Syndrome, or constantly chasing the newest innovations, must be avoided. It is crucial to understand what impact new technologies will have on consumer behavior to estimate its significance and decide whether or not to incorporate it into company or brand strategy. Only then does innovation make sense.

Innovating solidity will become an important quality in any marketeer's state-of-the-art work. The Mad (Wo)Men of tomorrow will have to make sure that their brands and companies keep making the right choices in any circumstance, without jumping all over the place. Because thinking about what tomorrow might bring, even if it is just for a little while, is enough to make your head spin.

Just imagine…

It is Thursday. You have just arranged to go for dinner with the love of your life, like you do each Friday. It is always the same restaurant. The food is great. The wine is great. After all those years the chef has become a friend. You blindly trust his cooking skills.

You: 'Hey Alexa. Can you book our restaurant for tomorrow?'
Alexa: 'I've made a reservation for19:30. Is that ok?'
You: 'That's fine, Alexa'.
Alexa: 'I see that the restaurant offers a new menu. The Autumn menu. It is 54 euros per person, wine included. Shall I order for two?'
You: 'Yes, you can order for two, Alexa'.
Alexa: 'Ordered the Autumn menu for two. To arrive there tomorrow at 19:30, you will have to leave at 18:45. Shall I order a ride?'

You do not own a car anymore, you see. Whenever you want to go somewhere, you call one. Well, your personal assistant does, you do not do it yourself. You ask Siri, Alexa, Google or Cortana. During the ride you do not even have to pay attention to traffic, the car drives itself. During the ride you can watch a movie, work or play a game.

Twenty minutes before your car arrives, Alexa tells you it is time to get ready. Alexa is everywhere. In your house, your phone, your computer, your car and your smart watch. Alexa knows that you need twenty minutes to get ready. It works: both of you are ready in time. In the car Alexa asks you what you would like to do. It is a 45 minute drive. Alexa knows that you have a subscription to Netflix and that *Narcos* is your favorite series. You did not see the last episode yet. It takes 55 minutes, though, just a tad too long. Maybe you would like to start watching? Would you rather hear the news headlines? Or listen to your playlist of preference on Spotify?

Nothing of the sort. What you actually want, is just to calmly chat with your partner. The self-driving car has quickly become one of your ideal places to talk. You discuss your plans for the weekend. Tomorrow your daughter is coming to visit. She is coming over by train. Has a car been ordered to pick her up? Check. What are we having for dinner? Pasta all'arrabbiata of course, it is her favorite. Wait, do we have the ingredients for it? 'Alexa, do we have everything to make pasta all'arrabiata?' Oh no, no tomatoes or cheese. Alexa is of course checking your smart fridge. Will she order it? From Tesco, as per usual? Oh, but the eggs are out as well. And the water. Maybe she can just order what she orders every Saturday, plus the tomatoes and the cheese?

Just like we did not have a crystal ball at the beginning of the internet revolution, and we could not foresee how important the internet would become, we lack one now to see the effect of AI and other upcoming technologies. We have to know them all, these novelties. We have to try them all ourselves, but let us avoid the shiny new object syndrome. Not all new technologies are equally important.

Today's advantage is that, compared to twenty years ago, we know better which direction to look at. Considering only our trade, digital technology has, first of all, brought us a number of large new media platforms. Some of these are controlled by us, some of them are completely out of our control. Secondly, digital technology has given us the opportunity to automate the distribution of our content on these media platforms. Thirdly, it has brought us more insights into the types of content we need to create, by generating data. To come up with content, we still need to rely on the human brain rather than an artificial brain, but as we have seen, even when it comes to this we are now testing the limits. Keeping a close eye on the innovations in media platforms, in the ways of automating content distribution and in the ways of gathering data to feed our insights and make better content, seems to be the best strategy today.

ERASE DIGITAL

In a world running on a new operating system, the new reality is the new normal. The new normal is that we, today, are living in a digital world. That is abundantly clear. Yet, we marketeers are still talking about digital marketing. However, in a digital world, it is no longer about traditional or digital marketing. It is about marketing in a digital world. There is no need for a distinction between digital or non-digital anymore. That is so last century. Or should I say last year? Instead, let us just do marketing and focus on the primary task of our trade: creating sustainable growth for our brands by seducing our consumers the right way. The best way to do so, will be discussed in detail when we explain the TapForward Model.

CHAPTER 2

ADVERTISING HAS TO ADJUST TO THE NEW OPERATING SYSTEM AS WELL

'THERE IS NOTHING PERMANENT EXCEPT CHANGE'

HERACLITUS

The Bowling Green Park in New York is known for Wall Street's Charging Bull statue, a Christmas present given to the inhabitants of the city in 1989. It was supposed to cheer up the New Yorkers in times of financial trouble. The Dow Jones Industrial Average had just crashed by an alarming 22%. The ferocious-looking bull was a symbol for the optimism and strength needed to turn the tide.

The 'Fearless Girl' statue (Source: *New York Times*)

It is Monday night, the 7th of March 2017. In the dark, a production team stops at Bowling Green park. It places a new statue, right in front of the Charging Bull, of a young girl undauntedly looking at the creature, hands on her sides. It completely changes the symbolism of the bull, now looking to charge and attack the little girl. Suddenly the animal stands for the machismo on Wall Street, the young girl for female leadership in the world of business.[15] The day after is International Women's Day. If all goes to plan, the action is bound to get a lot of attention.

The statue is called Fearless Girl and was commissioned by State Street Global Advisors, an investment agency from Boston. Not a small one either, the company controls 2.5 trillion dollars worth of assets and has existed for 225 years. With this initiative, it is not just looking to support International Women's Day but also wants to make a call for companies to include more women in the executive leadership teams. Their research proves time and time again that having more women at the top has a positive influence on the overall results of a company. To further enforce their argument, they launched the Gender Diversity Index, a listed fund that only invests in companies in which the majority of people in management are women. The stock symbol of the fund becomes SHE.[16] The company is allowed to leave the statue there for two days, hoping to attract as much attention as possible for the cause as well as their fund.

And attention it certainly gets. The world swoons for the little girl. She gains public support from prominent business women as well as from the mayor of New York. The press dedicates a lot of attention to the whole ordeal and the statue becomes a tourist attraction, a must-have selfie moment. In the next twelve weeks, the statue is shared 4.6 billion times on Twitter and 745 million times on Instagram.[17] It is mentioned 3,500 times on TV and 2400 articles about it appear (of which 96% neutral or positive). In total, the value of all the attention is estimated at 7.4 million dollars.[18] The financial results are astounding as well: in the first three days after the launch of the SHE fund, the daily trafficked volume increases by 384%. In the first four weeks, fifteen times more investors inquire about the initiative than before. Thirteen weeks after the launch, the fund's assets have grown by 8%. The impact on the company's employees are not to be underestimated either. Stephen Tisdalle, Chief Marketing Officer of the enterprise, summarized it as follows: 'It changed the way we are thinking about ourselves and what we represent.'

Although the statue could originally only stay for two days, New York City mayor Bill de Blasio announced it could stay through February 2018 after 40,000 people signed a petition asking that Fearless Girl become a permanent fixture on Wall Street. After that it would have to find a new home. It is still there.

Why was this campaign so successful? With a simple, yet powerful idea it managed to present a socially relevant cause in a way that profoundly touched people. And what do people do when something like that happens to them? They talk about it and share their experience with friends. In the past, this was limited to the bar around the corner. Today, it happens on social media all over the world. Basically the same thing, but on a mega scale, allowing the campaign to become way bigger than the allocated budget could ever have allowed. The campaign becomes 'famous' as it were. Once they reach this phase, marketeers can just sit back and enjoy. This is a law, a certainty. One we will return to a couple of times as we continue.

Advertising can still do it: baffle the world with an idea, make the public embrace a message, make a company famous overnight, align all of the people within a company. Unfortunately, most campaigns do not have the power of Fearless Girl. This campaign was indeed exceptional. Most advertisements lack the multiplier effect and never become famous. This is partly because the consumer has found a multitude of ways to avoid contact with advertising: recording their TV shows so they can fast forward through the breaks, skipping to a different channel when commercials do pop up, binge-watching Netflix without any commercial breaks at all. They install ad blockers to avoid banners on the web, maybe even unnecessarily, since we are increasingly 'suffering' from 'banner blindness'. And when watching a YouTube video, we will just impatiently wait to quickly press the *skip this ad* button.

Advertising seems, in most cases, nothing more than empty promises coming together in a tiny square that takes up too much space on our screens. Far-fetched exaggerations packed into six-second clips. Noise we try to avoid seeing or hearing at all costs. And the more our world digitalises, the more ways we get to avoid advertisements. 92% of ads do not get noticed anymore.[19]

So how is advertising doing? Not too well, you might think. Then again, maybe this is normal for the transformational phase we are living in today. We have to adjust to the new operating system. That takes time and true vision. One thing we have already learned, is that we need to deliver better work. Consumers are ruthless. The more mediocre commercials we throw at them, the more ad blockers will be installed, the more breaks will be skipped. Good work gets rewarded by the multiplier effect or the TapForward effect, more on which will be discussed later on. These effects increase campaign payoffs to more than the initial budget would allow, just like the story of the SHE fund.

This contradiction has always been there, but less black and white. In the past, consumers did not have access to the same means they have today to avoid our work. Digital has taken out the grey zone and made the choice for the consumer very clear: we are in or out. Average work does not get seen anymore. Strong work, good work, is awarded the TapForward treatment.

THE WATERCOOLER EFFECT

Those of us born in the '90s or later probably cannot even imagine there was a time when the launch of new campaigns from brands like Coca-Cola, Nike or Benetton was just as exciting as the launch of a new iPhone. New TV commercials were intensively discussed the day after at the water cooler or the coffee machine. It even had a name: The Watercooler effect, TapForward's predecessor. When this would happen, we knew it was a good campaign, even having a chance to become a part of popular culture. If that happened, we could be 100% certain that sales would benefit.

The Watercooler effect has its origins in the television industry. TV shows have a weekly rhythm. Viewers have to wait a week to watch the next episode, so it is the producer's responsibility to make sure that they make the viewer's attention last throughout the week. One way to do that, is to make them talk about it. Because the more people talk, the more important the show becomes and the more it gains a 'must-watch' status. Existing fans will loyally settle in before their TVs, as well as some new viewers, not wanting to miss out on the must-watch show.

Television producers have several techniques to get people talking: cliffhangers, plot twists, spectacular scenery, deep emotional occurrences. The goal is clear: this needs to be the next conversation at the watercooler. The more this is the case, the bigger the Watercooler effect and the greater the must-watch status of a show. Why is this relevant to us? Well, the same goes for advertising campaigns. Get people talking about it, then they will make the campaign work for us. Just like TV producers we also have techniques to get people talking. We will get back to those when discussing our new model. But first, let us take a look at a campaign from the '90s that had a huge Watercooler effect.

In July 1997, Lee Clow, Executive Creative Director of the American Advertising Agency TBWA/Chiat/Day, gets a phone call from Steve Jobs. Is he able to fly over? Jobs has something to discuss.[20] Steve Jobs has just returned to Apple as interim CEO after being fired in 1985. Apple is not doing well. If Jobs cannot turn it around quickly, the company will go bust. He starts a big clean-up: 70% of products are cancelled, four are left. All hope rests on the iMac, the multi-coloured all-in-one desktop computer. However, it is not ready yet and will not be until August 1998, more than a year later. Apple needs to create some breathing room until its launch and with only a couple of months' worth of cash the impossible needs to happen: the consumer has to quickly buy more Apple products. Apple needs to make a statement, needs to show that it stepped out of the downward spiral and that it is returning to its former glory. But faith in Apple has dissipated and only few think the company will actually make it. If you own a Mac, you are pretty sure it is going to be your last. This all changed with Jobs' return: he brought new hope, even though it was not much. *Wired*'s June edition cover from 1997 made a fitting summary: it shows the Apple logo and one word: 'Pray'.[21]

Lee Clow quickly understands that the answer cannot be found in a regular advertising campaign. He has to come up with an idea so powerful it shakes people to their core and will make them fall in love with Apple all over again. He has to make sure people will want to buy Apple again and he needs to do so now. He has to make sure Apple users regain trust in the brand. Lee Clow has to come up with an idea that will, literally, make people think differently about Apple. To say there is a lot on the line, is an understatement.

On the 23rd of September, eight weeks after that first phone call, Jobs shows the new campaign at an internal Apple meeting. The campaign revolves around the phrase 'Think Different' and pays tribute to big thinkers that changed the world. The TV commercial shows twelve of them: there are people like Albert Einstein, Pablo Picasso, John Lennon and Maria Callas. A voice honours them: 'Here is to the crazy ones. The misfits. The rebels. The trouble-makers. The round pegs in square holes. The ones who see things differently. They are not fond of rules. And they have no respect for the status quo. You can quote them, disagree with them, glorify or vilify them. About the only thing you cannot do is ignore them. Because they change things. They push the human race forward. And while some may see them as the crazy ones, we see genius. Because the people who are crazy enough to think they can change the world, are the ones who do. Apple, Think Different.'[22]

Seeing the commercial for the first time, goosebumps are guaranteed. Apple is back. So is Steve Jobs, the commercial obviously carrying his signature. A collective sigh is exclaimed by all Apple fans. It is the first public statement from Apple since Jobs return and it emits such confidence, such certainty that everything will be fine. However, most of all, it is the biggest ode to its consumers Jobs ever made. It is his way to say thank you: thank you for your support during these hard times.

The campaign works. It is fervently discussed at watercoolers and coffee machines. So much so, that in April of 1998 Apple turns a profit two quarters in a row. Its market share rises to 4.1%.[23] There are not any new products yet, so solely the Think Different campaign was moving people to buy more of the existing products. The campaign keeps going until 2002 and goes down in history as one of the most successful campaigns of the 20th century.

THE TAPFORWARD EFFECT

The Gorilla Advertisement from British confectionery factory Cadbury is another good example of what the Watercooler effect can do. Or is this the TapForward effect already? It is 2007 at this point and we are increasingly sharing things on social media instead of around the coffee machine.

For those who are not familiar with it, Cadbury's Dairy Milk chocolate is to the UK what Nutella is to the world. The brand has been around forever, it is the reference for all other chocolate brands and the eternal market leader. However, in 2007, Dairy Milk was going into its third year of negative growth. The traditional growth solutions for FMCG (Fast Moving Consumer Goods), expanding the product supply or organizing promotions, were not working anymore. The company is losing its connection with the younger consumer. They are not growing up with Cadbury like previous generations did, there are too many alternatives. Moreover, it is not just a short-term problem, it will have an even bigger impact in the long run. When these young people buy other brands when they become parents, Cadbury's market share will inevitably keep shrinking. To top it off, there is a salmonella problem: the brand has to call back a million of its products, costing them another 14% in sales.[24]

Cadbury needs to get their business back on track. The company needs to show that it is still alive and kicking. It needs to make sure that the brand preference grows, especially among young consumers. If Cadbury were a rock band, we would say it was time for a comeback. Not just any comeback however, a comeback that propels the group to the top of the charts and makes millions of fans remember why they became fans in the first place – and why they still are. It needs its fans to sing from the top of their lungs, convincing other people to become fans as well. No easy feat.

On the 31st of August 2007 the new campaign is aired for the first time. It builds up like a film, starting with an intriguing close-up of a gorilla. You hear the first tones of 'In the Air Tonight' by British pop singer Phil Collins. The gorilla closes his eyes and takes a deep breath. He is focusing. The camera pans out. There is an amplifier in the background. Out of focus, but you can see the outline. Are we in a recording studio? With a gorilla? He moves his neck left and right, popping it. He is ready. The camera pans out again. The gorilla is sitting behind a drumming kit. Another deep breath. As the iconic drumming intro of Phil Collins starts, so does he. He plays Phil Collins' piece. Doing it with the flair, the power and the confidence of a professional drummer. A couple of hits later, the screen turns purple and the Dairy Milk bar appears.

This was completely unprecedented. Cadbury usually made riskless videos containing loads of shots of people enjoying chocolate. So the company is now taking a risk, but it pays off. In three weeks, the clip gets ten million views on YouTube. Keep in mind that this is 2007: YouTube is only two years old. More than seventy Facebook groups are created around the commercial, uniting more than fifty thousand members. Hundreds of consumers are putting images of the clip online with other music in the background. 'In the Air Tonight' rises to number seventeen on the charts. The TapForward effect (letting people react, share, like, tweet, repost and parody on digital platforms) is obviously working.

The campaign is also a commercial success. The sales rise by 5.9% in the first month after the start. Almost 4 million young consumers buy their first Cadbury bar.[25] The downward trend has stopped, even greater, growth has returned for the company's.

THE TAPFORWARD EFFECT AND SALES

The bigger the TapForward effect, the stronger the rise in sales. Does this really correlate? Most definitely, and it has to do with the extra reach the effect brings along. It has been proven many times: there is a clear correlation between a campaign's reach and sales. British research confirmed it once more in 2017: 'The more people you reach within your target market, the bigger the effects on sales and profit tend to be.'[26]

We successfully realize this extra reach, when we get our consumers to react to our campaign in the pub, at home on the sofa or on social media. The more people react, the bigger the reach of our campaign becomes. In many cases we can get to a multiple of what we could have reached with our original budget.

Take Fearless Girl. The original budget was about 250,000 dollars, a budget that will not reach far.[27] The TapForward effect generated an extra 7.4 million dollars worth of media. That is almost thirty times as much, paired with a way bigger reach. Of course, that sort of success is not attainable for just any campaign.

Most campaigns will not notice a thing of the TapForward effect, because they will not succeed in activating it. It is more of an art than a science. However, if we analyze the campaigns that were lucky enough to obtain the effect, we will notice they share certain qualities. We will get back to those when building our new model, one that can face the challenges of the 21st century head on.

THE TAPFORWARD EFFECT
AND THE NEW OPERATING SYSTEM

The Watercooler effect of the past was important, but it did not have the power of TapForward given that its engine of worldwide social platforms simply did not exist yet. Today however, social media are a fundamental part of the new operating system.

Then again, it has never been easier to avoid commercials and advertisements. When we are watching on-demand or watching recordings, chances are that we will be skipping the commercial breaks and, on the internet, we will be blocking banners. This is also a part of the new operating system.

What it comes down to, is this: mediocre work does not fare well in the new operating system. It gets blocked or skipped. Quality work on the other hand, gets rewarded with a lot of energy and a way bigger reach, resulting in a way more positive effect on sales. Quality pays off, faster and more than before. Delivering good work and searching for the TapForward effect is now an essential part of making advertisements. Or so it should be!

Juniors starting in the advertising industry today, might not even be aware of this. Young marketeers are growing up in the world of Google and Facebook and know like no one else how to play with these platforms. They talk about contact points, zero moments of truth, ad depth, performance marketing and conversions. Not entirely unjustified, because this is an important part of our trade. These things create short-term results. It is digital sales activation, but this alone does not suffice. We must aim for sustainable growth, something we can only reach in combination with brand building. The 60/40 rule (60% of advertising budgets has to go to brand building, 40% to short-term sales activation) shows us the most efficient balance between the two.

If these young marketeers do not feel at ease in a world of brand building, activating the TapForward effect and focusing on long-term growth, they are not to blame. We are. We are not paying enough attention to training our young Mad (Wo)Men. We are not teaching them the fundamentals of the trade. Isaac Newton said in 1675: 'If I have seen further, it is by standing on the shoulders of the giants.'[28] Young marketeers do not know the giants of our trade anymore, so they cannot stand on their shoulders.

It is high time we explain to our young Mad (Wo)Men that Fearless Girl, Think Different and Real Beauty are a very important part of what we do, if not the most important part. Tell them that the real essence of our trade can be recognized in the Watercooler effect or the contemporary version of this: the TapForward effect. And that this effect is the key to sustainable growth, in combination with short-term sales conversion. That is the ambition we have to share with them. As the saying goes: 'Aim at the stars. If you miss, you'll still land on the moon.' And landing on the moon is already way better than what we are achieving with most of our campaigns today. We are not even able to get them to take off.

PROGRAMMATIC ADVERTISING

In July 2017, two reports on the advertising industry are published. Both written by financial analysts. On the one hand Charles Bedouelle from BNP Paribas and on the other hand Brian Wieser of equity research company Pivotal Research Group. Both have been following the industry for a long time. One is from America, the other from Europe. Both give the industry a bad grade, hitting them where it hurts.

The industry is not adapting fast enough to the new operating system. Doubts are growing as to whether or not the big advertisement companies will be able to deliver their growth forecasts. The analysts see too much disruption and too slow of a reaction speed. They see brands looking more and more for cost reduction and efficiency, putting pressure on the revenues of their advertising agencies. They see upcoming competitors, to which the industry is only reacting hesitantly. They see a growing automatization in the planning and buying of media. This makes for a reduction in costs, but also for a *flou artistique* or a vagueness when it comes to actual results. Let us take a look at the rising automatization of media planning and buying. Because software is indeed increasingly deciding where ads appear.

It is called programmatic advertising and it is fundamentally connected to the new operating system. It is about automating the process of buying media. The goal is clear: through automation, efficiency goes up and costs go down. It works like this: we put the goals, the consumer data and the chosen advertising formats into a programmatic buying platform. With a click or a press on the button the algorithm gets started. In the milliseconds before a page loads on a screen, a virtual auction takes place. The buying platforms bid for the chance to place an advertiser's advert on it, based on consumer data: where a consumer lives, whether he or she is young or old, recently shopped for food or searched for a new mobile phone. We even might create multiple ads and serve different executions to different slices of the audience. Based on the results and real time feedback, the algorithm will adjust the strategy and media choice appropriately. This process gets repeated over and over again, without any human intervention. In other words: programmatic advertising allows efficient, large scale spreading of digital advertising campaigns.

Especially international brands benefit from this large scale. Since they are selling all over the world, they also need to reach the whole world. Because it is automated, programmatic advertising platforms offer a productivity humans cannot realize anymore. And because it is based on consumer data it is believed to be more effective. The algorithm tries to reach a certain audience. It is not interested in the context in which the ads will appear. That is why we talk about audience planning more than media planning.

However, this method has its flaws. Because they understand that reach is lacking, online players are creating advertising space wherever they can. Some go overboard: for some, even a pixel of free space can be put on sale as advertising space. This has led to our current situation, in which we are getting an overdose of digital ads, prompting the consumer to start blocking them. So, it is for our own benefit, to reign ourselves in and start offering more quality advertising spaces.

A second flaw is the lack of information about the websites or pages the ads are eventually published on. We have no idea in what sort of context our content is appearing. This makes things go very wrong sometimes. *The Times*, in March of 2017, noticed that some ads by prominent brands were being placed next to YouTube videos supporting hate messages, terrorism or anti-Semitism.[29] And this does not seem to be a solely British problem. *The Wall Street Journal* has found some examples in the US as well. Google apologized immediately. A few big brands (GM, PepsiCo, Walmart, M&S, BBC, …) pulled their advertising budgets even faster. No one wants their advertising to be seen on a page with videos by hate preachers. This is about brand safety: in no way do brands want to be associated with improper practices.

If you look at it with a broader perspective it is also about context. Currently, advertisers seem to care more about targeting the right audience that placing their ads in the right, qualitative context. Does it really matter where people see your ads? It does. Research recently published in *Admap Magazine* shows that context makes a significant difference for whether an ad gets noticed or engaged with. It also reveals a strong correlation between ads that gets noticed and sales conversions when the ads get shown in a qualitative environment. Targeting the right audience is important but it is even more important to target them in the right context.

A third flaw is fraud. Just like media companies are plagued by fake news (for example Facebook during the 2016 US presidential elections), so is programmatic advertising plagued by fraudulent advertisements. This takes on a multitude of shapes and forms, one of which is fraud concerning search terms. Malevolent people build sites full of precious search terms to generate ads and reap income. Ad stacking is a method where banners are stacked on top of each other. Of course, only the top one is visible for the visitor, but one visit counts as a viewing of all of the ads. We are paying for an impression of an ad no one has seen. Sometimes visitors are not even human anymore, but bots, bits of software programmed to click banners, generating fake clicks.

Then there is spoofing: frauds buy cheap media space on low quality websites but offer these spaces on ad exchanges as if they were high quality like cnn. com, cbs.com, etc. Your ads of course never end up on these sites. In 2016, about 7.2 billion dollars were lost to these types of advertising fraud.[30] This made up about 3% of the budget that brands spent in total on their advertising. According to JPMorgan Chase advertisers lost 16.4 billion dollars to digital ad fraud in 2017. Enough to take serious action.

Take into account the complicated chain of value of programmatic advertising as well. A lot of parties are taking their share of the earnings: trading desks, DSPs, ad exchanges, ad networks, SSPs, making it difficult to understand who does what and who earns what. This leads to a lack of transparency.

To top it all off, it turns out that not all of the results are correct. Facebook had to admit in September 2016 that it has been reporting false statistics on the amount of views a video gets since 2014.[31] In November that year, it had to confess to some other mistakes. In 2018 the data analytics firm Cambridge Analytica was accused of using personal information harvested from more than 50 million Facebook profiles without permission to build a system that targeted US voters with personalized political advertisements based on their psychological profile. Mark Zuckerberg needed to apologize again and promised to prevent it from happening again. This, of course, is making everyone a bit nervous.

How we bring our campaigns to the public is, just like the creative content, key to their success. So, it is important that all these flaws get fixed as soon as possible. A couple of big advertisers are thinking the same way. Unilever and P&G have asked the industry to take responsibility and solve these problems, fast. If this does not happen, they are threatening to pull out their digital budgets. Research by Mediarader from June 2017, concludes that they are.[32] In 2017, P&G advertises on 33% less websites with a budget lowered by 41% compared to the year before. Unilevers budget went down by 59% and the total number of websites by 11%.

When a giant like P&G speaks, the industry listens. In March 2017 Marc Pritchard, P&G's Chief Brand Officer gave a speech on the ANA Media Masters Conference in Orlando.[33] It is regarded as the most important speech of this generation of marketeers. Pritchard counters the digital bombing of consumers in diverse formats, that has only resulted in a rise in adblock users instead of in sales. He wants more quality, transparency, brand safety and is showing zero tolerance against advertising fraud.

A month later he mentions this again in another speech in Los Angeles.[34] He talks about the 'crap trap': we are creating so many bad ads that we are only pushing consumers away from our products. 'If legends like Leo Burnett and David Ogilvy were to come back and observe our behavior today, what would they think we believe about advertising? Our behavior indicates we believe more is better. We bombard consumers with thousands of ads a day. We are awfully busy, but all of this activity is not breaking through the clutter. It is just creating more noise.'[35] He even has the numbers to prove it: in July 2017, P&G announces that the company has saved more than 100 million dollars on digital advertising in the second quarter of the year. More importantly, it has had no effect on the number of sales. That keeps growing anyhow. Jon Moeller's conclusion, the CFO of P&G, 'is that the spending we cut was largely ineffective'.[36] Because of too much crap, bots and fake clicks.

'Is this all going to end well?', we could ask yourself. Of course, it is. None of the involved parties can afford to ignore these problems. *The Drum*, the British specialized advertising journal, organizes a Prediction Panel every year with representatives from our industry. During the panel of December 2017, there at least seemed to be a consensus on what needed to happen. Ad fraud, viewability, brand safety: it all needs to be handled and solved in 2018.[37] So, it seems we have woken up.

The government is playing its part as well. With the GDPR (General Data Protection Regulation) the European Union designed a new framework for data protection. This put the control back into the hands of the consumer and helps us deal with data in a more transparent, safe and respectful way. The first result is that a lot of companies have seen their database of consumers shrink drastically. Which only means that the content they were sharing with their consumers was not good enough anyway. It forces them to create more qualitative content if they want to reconnect with their consumers. Which is a good thing not only for consumers, but also for our industry. Not only did advertisers see their database shrink, also the programmatic platforms now have less data available for audience planning which increases the importance of context or choice of media. Which is also a good thing for our industry.

MATH (WO)MEN

We are creating huge amounts of data. In 2015 we generated 0.77 gigabytes per person daily.[38] That amounts to 2,500,000,0000,000,000,000 bytes a day. The equivalent of 10 million Blu-ray discs. According to IDC, the ICT market researching bureau, we will be creating 180 zettabytes of data per year in 2025. This means the number 180 followed by twenty-one zeroes. If we wanted to send all this data over a broadband connection, it would take 450 million years.[39] Safe to say we can take the term 'big data' literally.

So, what are we supposed to do with this mass of data? If we should believe data-analysts, then this is the wet dream of every marketeer turned into reality: thanks to data, we can offer every consumer a perfectly personalized proposal. But maybe that is a little bit overenthusiastic. At least for now. A recent poll found that 70% of consumers regard most forms of personalized marketing as 'creepy'.

What does seem within reach is what P&G calls Mass one-on-one Marketing. Pritchard launched the concept in September 2017 during a speech at Dm-exco, the international exhibition and conference of the digital industry.[40] It seems a contradiction, mass one-on-one marketing. An example however clarifies what P&G means. Take Pampers. The moment a future mom starts to look for information about pregnancies on Google, Pampers gets the signal that someone is starting the pregnancy journey. From that moment on, the mom gets to see Pampers' content, helping her through her pregnancy. When the baby is born, Pampers tells her what the different types of diapers are for. And so on. The brand spreads a message handmade for moms. A lot of moms. Hence the concept mass one-to-one.

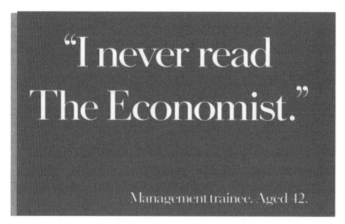

An iconic advert by *The Economist* (Source: *The Economist*)

P&G is of course not the only company that sees the advantages of data in making advertisements more relevant. *The Economist* noticed these examples as well. Data was the foundation of a very successful worldwide recruitment campaign. This evolution shows that the Mad (Wo)Men of today also are Math (Wo)Men, embracing the possibilities of data and forging it together with a big chunk of creativity.

The Economist has been the leading magazine in the business world for years, with high-quality articles. The campaign that *The Economist* has been running for the past twenty years is a classic. It is a clever campaign with intelligent headlines on an iconic red background. However, it has one disadvantage: many people in the business world assume that the magazine is out of their reach. That the brand is not relevant for them. This is diluting the circulation. Loyal readers are getting older, while the younger crowd is not interested. For them, it is an old-fashioned magazine, probably filled with way too complicated articles. However, if you show them a copy, their opinion changes. Suddenly they understand the journalistic value the magazine brings: accessibility, open-mindedness, it is progressive, surprising, intelligent and looks beyond the business world. Especially that last element is important, because what the younger crowd is interested in, the so-called 'progressives', is an intelligent view of the world. The whole world.

A new campaign has to adjust this perception of *The Economist*. If the journal wants to get its circulation to grow, then it needs to sell nine thousand subscriptions, worldwide. This is the goal of the campaign in addition to defining a group of 650,000 people to retarget. With a budget of 2 million pounds for a worldwide campaign, all the company can get is a worldwide online-banner campaign. However, knowing the problem of banner blindness, the magazine will have to use an interesting and creative twist. It decides to use the power of programmatic advertising, given that is the fastest way to get the banners to appear on the websites of the progressives.

The campaign starts a couple of hours after the American senators publish their report on the torture practices by the CIA. *The Economist* posts a banner on CNN reporting on the matter, which reads 'CIA torture'. If you click it, you will end up reading an article by *The Economist*. The creative strategy is clear: use banners to quickly and intriguingly react to current occurrences. Sufficiently intriguing to seduce the reader to click on it and to end up on an editorial of *The Economist*.

Another example is a banner with the message: 'Have American cops gone ballistic?' The ad appeared on webpages reporting on the riots in Ferguson in August 2014.

The Economist's 'Raising Eyebrows' campaign by The Economist (Source: warc.com)

The Economist also offers summaries of news-items, each about ten seconds long, in a quick-read style. To be able to publish these quickly, the magazine set up a newsroom in direct contact with its editors. As soon as they approve an article, the newsroom puts the ad online.

Given the small budget and the worldwide ambitions, the magazine has to make sure that the banners are only visible to the right readers, with content that is as best suited to them as possible. To do so, they analyze the reading behavior of some of their most active readers on their website. Seven fields of interest are identified, lookalikes (people with the same characteristics as the target audience) are formed. Technology for contextual targeting is used to scan what the group is reading, and based on this, dynamic advertising is sent to them. A database of more than a hundred potential banners is created.

The result of this campaign? 64,405 new subscriptions. Far exceeding the set goal of 9,000. Their other goal, defining a group of 650,000 prospects to re-target after the campaign, was surpassed as well: the group counts 5.2 million people. In total, the campaign raked in 51.7 million pounds, with a total cost of 2 million. Good for a 25:1 ratio.

Data is allowing us to work extremely efficiently. Unlike the campaigns we discussed before, this campaign does not count on the FastForward effect. That would be the wrong strategy in this case. *The Economist* needed to work as structured and close-knitted as possible, in order to reach the right people on a global scale. Again: a good example that shows how programmatic advertising, consumer-data and creativity can enforce each other to achieve a good result.

STOP THE CONFUSION

Everyone has an opinion about the future of our trade and does not refrain from throwing it all over the internet. It is good to hear different opinions, it feeds the debate. However, we all know opinions are worth a lot more when they are actually based on facts and data. Unfortunately, unfounded yelling and screaming happens to be more noticeable than well-grounded opinions. This results in confusion, just the thing that we do not need in this time of transformation. We need to stop this confusion, because it is distracting us from what truly matters. David Ogilvy already said it in the sixties: 'Your role is to sell, do not let anything distract yourself from the sole purpose of advertising.'[41]

Let us apply Simon Sinek's Golden Circle to find out what our job really is:

The **why** of what we do is simple: advertising is meant to sell products. Preferably more than before and kept up on a long-term basis. In other words: the goal is to create sustainable growth. No matter how technology changes the world, as long as we are working in the current capitalistic system, creating sustainable growth will be the goal of most brands.

The **what** is clear as well: making content. Building brands with content on one hand and activating sales on the other. Again, it does not matter how things are changing. As long as we need to influence people, we need to speak to them. In order to do so, we need to create content. Will we have to adapt the content to new platforms? Of course, television brought the thirty-second format, digital has brought the six-second format. But this only changes our canvas, our carrier, it has nothing to do with whether we need content to generate sustainable growth.

How can we bring these campaigns to our consumers? Through media platforms, either owned, earned or paid. And this is where technology comes in. This is where the disruption is happening. And this is where the confusion is.

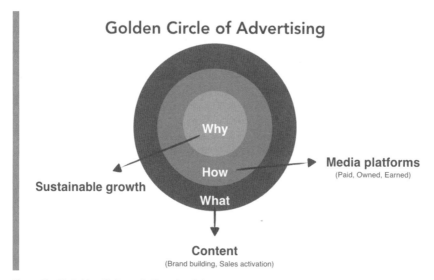

Simon Sinek's Golden Circle applied to advertising

WHEN SOMETHING NEW COMES ALONG, WE DECLARE THE OLD FOR DEAD

As the Mad (Wo)Men we are, we adore innovation. That makes sense, as we have to know what the next new mainstream thing will be, long before it actually breaks through. However, we have the annoying tendency to, once we know of the new thing, to drop the old one immediately. Stronger yet, we declare them dead. When television broke through, we declared cinema dead. It is still there. Television was quite devilish actually, it was going to kill the radio as well, yet we still listen to it. By now we should realize that the new never truly replaces the old. The old medium can become less important, but it is never entirely wiped away. It still remains next to the new.

The debate on the state of the TV commercial on Google (Source: Google)

Ever since the internet went mainstream, we have been doing the same with the TV-commercials. For years. If we were to believe Google's search results, we have been doubting the survival of the television commercials ever since 2011. By 2015 we were sure: the TV-commercial is dead. In 2016 it was reconfirmed: it is still dead. Hold on, what did we read in 2017? It is not dead at all. Come again?

The TV-commercial is indeed not dead. In fact, it is still the most efficient format for advertising. Compared to other traditional and digital media, TV advertising generates 62% of all advertisement generating revenue on a short-term and 72% on a long-term basis. These are very recent numbers, published in November 2017 by British researching-website WARC.[42] Many people find these results peculiar, because they clash with the general perception in our industry today.

However, there is more: the same research shows that TV holds the biggest ROI compared to other forms of media. Per invested pound, TV delivers 4.2. Another confusing fact.

Does this mean that television is not fussed in the slightest by the commercials being skipped by their viewers? Not at all. Does it mean that Netflix has had no effect on the viewing behavior? Again, no. It only means that the facts today show that TV is doing better as an advertising carrier than any other medium. Nothing more, but also nothing less.

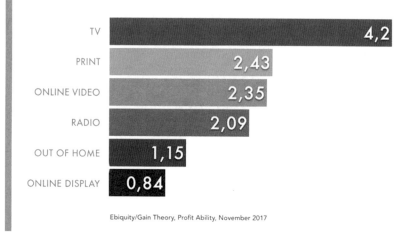

Average ad-generated total profit return over 3 years (£)

TV	4,2
PRINT	2,43
ONLINE VIDEO	2,35
RADIO	2,09
OUT OF HOME	1,15
ONLINE DISPLAY	0,84

Ebiquity/Gain Theory, Profit Ability, November 2017

ROI per media channel (Source: warc.com)

The real problem is that by now, we have heard TV is dead so many times, we have started to believe it ourselves. So much so, that a part of us even resists these results. It just cannot be true, the numbers are wrong. Confusion everywhere: TV ought to be the least effective of all traditional media. We have to get rid of this confusion, because understanding the real value of the different media channels is important. We cannot base our media selection on hunches or gut feelings, but only on hard numbers and facts.

WE ARE LIVING IN OUR OWN MEDIA-BUBBLES

Our media usage, that of the Mad (Wo)Men, cannot be compared to the way the average Joe uses media. We use it way more intensely. More than eight out of ten Mad (Wo)Men use WhatsApp, while the average WhatsApp usage rate does not reach 40%. Almost 70% of Mad (Wo)Men use Instagram, while the average usage rate amounts to 18%. More than six out of ten Mad (Wo)Men watch Netflix, for average Joe, this is three out of ten.

If you live your life on social media, it is difficult to imagine that other people do not. We live in our own media bubble, one that differs greatly from the average Joe's habitat. Sometimes we confuse them and make decisions based on our own experiences, rather than based on market numbers. This is influencing our decisions concerning the 'how'. Another thing to get rid of. We have to choose the most effective ways to bring our messages to our consumers. And if that means that we will have to drop that one Snapchat-based idea, well, so be it.

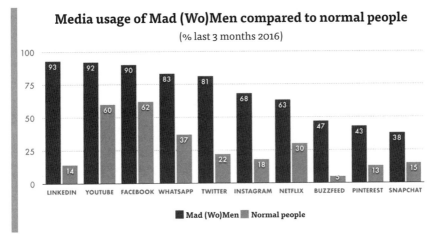

The Mad (Wo)Men's media bubble (Source: Thinkbox)

Combining the old and the new

How newspapers reacted to the radio broadcast of *The War of the Worlds* (Source: National Archives)

'If I would have planned to wreck my career, I could not have gone about it better', Orson Welles stated to a couple of journalists in 1938.[43] The night before, Welles and his Mercury Theatre On Air brought a radio-adaptation of *The War of the Worlds* on CBS Radio. *The War of the Worlds* is the story of an invasion of New Jersey by aliens, written forty years prior by H.G. Wells. The radio version, broadcasted the night before Halloween, sounds like a live reporting of the event. The warning at the beginning of the programme, saying all of the following is made up, was not heeded. A million Americans fell for the story. On Halloween, the papers are filled with stories of people having committed suicide to avoid falling into the hands of the invaders about mass bouts of panic in the streets of big cities. About thousands of New Yorkers fleeing their city or running off to New Jersey to see the invasion with their own eyes. Panicking people calling the police, the radio stations and the papers asking them what to do. If you can believe the papers, America seems to have suffered a short spell of mass hysteria.

In May 2016, the *Telegraph* set the story straight. There was no mass hysteria at all and there were no million Americans listening. The reporting appears to have been terribly overexaggerated, which was no coincidence. The papers were fighting a dire war against the then new medium over the advertising budgets of American companies. They jumped on the opportunity to blow up the whole ordeal, in order to teach the new medium a lesson. The editorial of the *New York Times*, just a day after the broadcast, stated: 'Radio is new but it has adult responsibilities. It has not mastered itself or the material it uses.'[44] In other words: radio is not to be trusted, so think twice before you spend your money on it. Who knows what it will do to your brand?

Today, there is no mass hysteria after a radio show, but there is a tough battle between the traditional media and the digital duopoly of Google and Facebook over the advertising budgets of the marketeers. On both sides, we are swarmed by arguments. Google and Facebook do want the advertising revenue, but not the responsibility traditional media has to carry, or so we hear. Why invest in TV if YouTube is stronger, the other party asks. The duopoly is refusing to let an independent party measure their results, because they are afraid to be compared to the results of traditional media, the latter one claims. There is no end.

We, the Mad (Wo)Men of today, must not allow ourselves to be dragged into this battle. Our concern is the true reality of the consumer. At the beginning of the book, we mentioned a model that would combine the old and the new. The same applies here: the reality of the consumer is telling us we do not have to choose a side, there is a need for both. Or maybe we do have to choose: we have to pick the side of efficiency. How will we bring our message to the consumer in the most cost-effective way? That is the question we need to answer.

The American consultancy bureau Bain & Company, which can hardly be accused of being biased in this debate, helps us answer this question. Their analysis shows that digital media are a less expensive means of reaching small groups of consumers. However, the percentage of people reached who remember the message stagnates at around 30%. Traditional media, and especially TV, are more expensive, but people tend to remember the advertisements: that number amounts to about 60%.[45] When they look at the sales intentions, that number rises to 80% for consumers who have seen the commercial in both traditional and digital media. So, the conclusion seems clear: it is not a matter of one or the other, it is about combining both.

The media choices of the digital companies themselves may illustrate this best. In 2016, Google invested 74% of their U.S.-advertising budget in TV.[46] In that same year, Facebook invested 59% of its budget in TV. In the UK, the online industry is the biggest spender in TV-advertising, followed by the food and the cosmetic industries.[47]

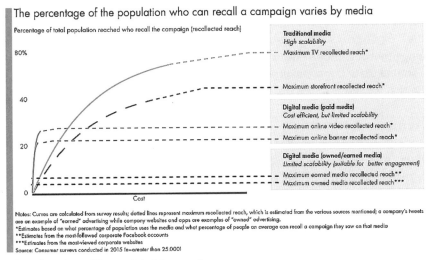

Ad Recall per channel (Source: Bain & Company)

ADJUSTING TO A NEW MEDIUM TAKES TIME

We have faced serious changes quite a few times already, especially in the media. After all, we must not forget that radio and television once were new media as well, just like Google, Facebook, YouTube and Instagram are today. The pattern still is the same. In the beginning, we try to apply what we know to the new medium. The first radio ads resembled spoken newspaper adverts.

The first television shows were just like radio, but with moving pictures. Next, we come to realize that it does not really work and we need to look for a more appropriate approach optimized for the new medium. The 30-second television commercial is a beautiful example of how we adjusted to TV when it was a new advertising medium.

In the first years of TV, commercial breaks did not exist. TV stations aired shows produced by advertising agencies commissioned by advertisers. The model worked for everyone. Towards the end of the '50s, broadcasters decided they wanted to make their own shows. The airtime for the advertisers was reduced to the commercial breaks, where one advertiser after the other got 30 seconds to sell their products.

You can imagine how big a change it was for the advertising agencies. Making 30-second commercials was an entirely new trade. The first years were like putting band-aids on wooden legs. The commercials were painfully long, sales pitches of sometimes up to two minutes. Filled to the brim with every possible argument you might think of to sell the product. Just take a look at the TV-commercial for Cadillac on YouTube.[48] It is nothing more than one long product demonstration. The Ford commercial tried, on its end, to sell a second car to homemakers.[49] As you will see, they were different times. Neither would air today.

We still needed time to understand how to make TV-commercials work, up until 1964, to be precise. It is Bill Bernbach who showed the way. In 1959, Carl Hahn, president of Volkswagen in the U.S., was looking for an advertising bureau to promote the Beetle. Not a simple feat: Americans love big, stylish cars with a lot of leg room and a big, big trunk. The Beetle is nothing less than the complete opposite. To top it all off: it is a German car, meaning Hitler plays a part in its conception. All in all: not really something the average American is waiting for. Hahn puts his faith in DDB (Doyle Dane Bernbach). The people from DDB figure out quickly that they need a different approach if they want the Beetle to have a chance in America. They find it. The commercial defines the beginning of the creative revolution in advertising (we will get back to it in a later chapter) and quickly became the standard for all to come.

The tale told is as brilliant as it is simple.[50] You see a man walking to his garage in the morning. It is still dark outside and the weather looks grim. He drives out of the garage in a Beetle on to a street completely covered in a thick layer of snow. The Beetle makes its way through. Suddenly you hear a voice: 'Have you ever wondered how the man who drives a snowplough, drives to the snowplough?' Meanwhile, the man arrives at a big hangar. 'This one drives a Volkswagen. So, you can stop wondering.' The gate opens, the man gets in and drives out with a huge snowplough. Through the snow, past the Beetle. A Beetle that looks quite small, next to the huge snowplough.

No word about the fact that the Beetle has the engine at the back so that it holds the road well. It is not necessary. The commercial says it in a much stronger way. Sir Alan Parker, praised British director and copywriter, once called it the simplest and most powerful commercial ever.[51] The MoMa added it to its permanent film collection. In 1999, on the international advertising Cannes Lions festival, it was elected the best TV commercial of the 20th century.[52]

So, it took a little over fifteen years before we mastered the art of the thirty-second commercial. And it has been twenty years since the internet took its first steps. We are ready!

TO THE MAD (WO)MEN OF TOMORROW

Our world is running on a new operating system. In other words, our trade is ready for a big renewal. We had twenty years to understand the digital revolution and its effects. Twenty years well spent, we have learned a lot already.

The new operating system brings a lot of opportunities. The TapForward effect is just one. Our best work can have a bigger and longer effect, both when it comes to brand building and when it comes to hard numbers. Cadbury's gorilla campaign was one of the very first campaigns to enjoy its full effect. The Fearless Girl campaign properly showed what the TapForward effect can do with an idea. A picture of a girl on a square in New York traveled around the world, powered only by this effect. In total, worth thirty times more than the original budget. So, it is worth it, crucial even, to understand perfectly how to activate this TapForward effect. We will get back to this later on.

Next to the TapForward effect, there is also the opportunity to combine our creativity together with data. *The Economist*'s campaign shows this beautifully. It was thanks to the new operating system and the clever use of data that the magazine managed to send its creative message to the right people, all over the world. And it paid off, big time. An ROI of 25:1. Merely with the right mixture of using data and programmatic advertising.

Thirty or twenty-five times what the budget could offer. That is unheard of. Today, it is within the reach of every Mad Man, given that we deliver good work and do not over complicate things. All of the confusion we are creating, is keeping us from thinking clearly. That, however, is just what we need to be able to deliver good work. So, let us snap out of it. Our trade is about simplifying things. Or to quote Marc Pritchard: 'Our trade is about a deep insight that translates into a great creative idea that translates into great sales'.[53]

CHAPTER 3

ON GIANTS' SHOULDERS

'THOSE THAT FAIL TO LEARN FROM HISTORY,

ARE DOOMED TO REPEAT IT'

WINSTON CHURCHILL

Every craftsman needs to know his history. Was it not Alexander McQueen, the British designer, who said: 'You got to know the rules to break them. That is why we are here: to demolish rules but keep tradition.'[54] Picasso was on the same page too: 'Learn the rules like a pro, so you can break them as an artist.'[55]

We just talked about our confusion. Every once in a while, we have difficulty distinguishing the 'how', the 'why' and the 'what' of our trade. And whenever we are talking about the 'how', we tend to always just agree with each other, sometimes collectively coming to the wrong conclusions.

On top of that, we also have the time-consuming tendency to want to reinvent the wheel. Influencer marketing for example, is nothing but a digital form of celebrity endorsement, invented in the beginning of the '50s. The most recent and well-known example is American actor George Clooney as a brand ambassador for Nespresso. We know that celebrity endorsements only work if they are supported by the halo effect. George Clooney is associated with certain qualities and through the halo effect, these qualities are projected on the Nespresso products. Knowing so makes it easy to understand that the use of micro influencers is being questioned. They do not have a halo effect, so why do we expect them to?

The role of content marketing (Source: Google)

The same goes for content marketing, which was invented at the end of the 19th century. Some of the content initiatives started back then have stood the test of time and are still used today. You would think that, after a hundred years, we would now understand what content marketing can and cannot do. Apparently not. Today, we are still debating whether content marketing is the new PR, the new sales activation tactic, a new form of Search Engine Marketing or the new branding...

We can name some other examples of techniques we keep reinventing. This confusion or ambiguity of imprecision makes it difficult to, as Picasso said, learn the rules and then improve them.

The giants of advertising preceded us and invented all the advertising techniques we know today. So, let us not reinvent the wheel. Let us stand on the shoulders of these giants so we can look even further and implement their techniques, with proper knowledge, into our new operating system, improving them where necessary.

We start our search for the giants of our industry at the end of the 19th century: the start of modern advertising. The industrial revolution is yielding its rewards. Big monuments are lit up at night, they get a touch of prestige to them and attract crowds of onlookers. Store windows are lighting up as well: for the very first time, you are able to see products in the dark. They look even more beautiful than by day.

The first cars appear in the street. A bit of a different sight compared to all of the horses. Different, but also dangerous. An American newspaper described cars as: 'tearing along the street at a lively rate'.[56] A lively rate of twenty miles an hour, in fact. Airplanes are appearing in the skies, vinyl records are filling houses with music. The phone has been invented, so now people can talk to family members at the other end of the country. But not only that. 'It saves letter writing, orders the dinner, invites the guests, reserves the tickets, and calls the carriage. It makes appointments, changes the time, cancels them altogether and renews them. It calls the expressman, calls the cab, and instructs the office.'[57] People are merely wondering who is listening in. It is a wondrous time. A time where everything is possible. Many entrepreneurs are bringing new products to the market and prove to be quite creative as well. A couple of their techniques still function today, even a hundred years after their conception. Just like content marketing.

In 1900, there are about three thousand cars driving around in France.[58] The country houses the most important car production in the world, producing a little over thirty thousand cars in 1905, almost 49% of the total global production. In the U.S., the total amount of produced cars is a little over eleven thousand.[59]

Driving a car back then was not a daily occurrence. There are no regulations and there are no traffic signs. There are routes, but no maps to keep track of them. You never know how long your journey will take or even whether you are driving in the right direction: there are no road signs. The maximum speed is 20 miles an hour. The roads are bad, dusty, not lit up and full of gravel. In other words, it was a risky endeavour to be driving into the countryside. The cars themselves are not very reliable either. And when they do, inevitably, break down, help is not easy to come by. You have to look for a mechanic or a phone. Not so easy, seeing as there were but 182,000 phone subscriptions in France in 1908.[60] Chances are that to find one, the driver has a long walk ahead of him.

These are the early days of the car industry. Not everyone, just like with any innovation, is convinced that cars will ever become a big thing. However, brothers Édouard and André Michelin are believers. Their grandfather owns a rubber-producing company. They turn it into a company that produces bicycle tyres in 1889. In those times, cycling was already quite a popular pastime.

The inspiration for their success can be traced back to an English cyclist, asking André to fix his tyre.[61] It was a pneumatic one, not a full one. The tyre filled with air is more comfortable because it holds the road better than a full tyre. It is also brand new: Dunlop only just invented it. The only disadvantage is that the tyre is glued to the wheel. It takes some time to fix the tyre, André needs three hours to fix it, plus another 6 hours until the tyre is fully glued to the frame and the Englishman can safely cycle again.[62]

Yet, the idea of a pneumatic car tyre had rooted itself in Andrés mind. However, unlike Dunlop, he made sure it did not need to be glued to the rim, calling for a simple design and an easy fix. The brothers wagered everything they had on the idea, having complete faith in the car as the most important means of transport for the future. And they were right: the car tyres sold like crazy. By 1900, they were leading the market in France.

At that moment in time, most of the cars in France were driven in Paris. Not very interesting for a tyre manufacturer. The cars did not drive very far, so the tyres did not wear out quickly. How could the brothers get people to drive greater distances? It is a matter for André, who is responsible for marketing while his brother ran the business. Over a hundred years ago, in his search, André Michelin laid the foundation of the first and most successful marketing case ever. A feat deserving the utmost respect.

André carefully watched the Touring Club de France (TCF), an organisation founded in 1890 to promote cycling and cyclo-tourism. The TCF had a monthly magazine for their members, giving all sorts of information for traveling through France by bike. They published maps, shared travel stories and developed specific cycling routes. This kind of thing interested André quite a bit. He wanted a guide of his own, the *Guide Michelin*, entirely focused on car tourism. Not a word about bicycles.

The first edition of the guide was published in 1900, on the occasion of the world expo in Paris.[63] The guide counted 399 pages and was printed 35,000 times in a small format, so it fitted in the drivers' pockets.

The guide was divided into three chapters and did not resemble the Michelin Guide we know today at all. It was more of a practical guide, with the first chapter being a manual for car tyres, explaining in great detail how to replace a tyre, inflate it, repair it or how to ask Michelin to do it for you. It also included a list of all the Michelin dealers in the country. In the summer, you could find dealers in 48 cities, compared to about six in the winter. Most are active in the South of France, to serve the bourgeoisie who spend their winters there. The car still was not the oiled machine we know today, it broke down constantly. If Andre and Édouard wanted people to travel through France, they had to make it abundantly clear that support was ubiquitous.

The second part of the *Guide Michelin* featured an overview of French cities and municipalities, though not including every town. The guide only showed those with a mechanic or a business selling fuel. Gas stations, like we know them today, did not exist back then. People bought fuel in grocery shops, drug stores, bicycle shops or from mechanics. This second part also contained a list of hotels. No restaurants just yet, unless they were part of a hotel. The guide did already rate every hotel, albeit roughly. Hotels with three stars offered a room, candles and three meals a day (with wine) for thirteen French francs. The two-star hotels had the same offering, but at a rate of ten to thirteen francs. The third category, with just one star, mentioned the hotels with a rate of less than ten francs.

The third and final chapter of the guide contained traffic rules and ads for French car producers and dealers in car parts. With a calendar, drivers could keep up with how many kilometres they had driven and how much fuel they had used. Or check up on the times for the sunrise and sunset, to avoid driving at night, after all: the roads were not yet lit.

The Michelin company was very aware that the content of the guide was not without its flaws and that it needed updating every year. They, again, found inspiration with the TCF, which asked its members to contribute. Michelin decided to do so as well. The introduction to the 1900 edition read: 'L'ouvrage se perfectionnera d'année en année, il sera parfait d'autant plus vite que les chauffeurs répondront plus soigneusement et en plus grand nombre au questionnaire.'[64]

The preface of the first Guide Michelin (Source: Chines & Puces)

The brothers asked their readers to check several things: the distance between two towns, the stock at the Michelin-dealers, whether the fuel-dealers had enough stock, the quality and the pricing of the hotels, the quality of the mechanic's workmanship and whether they could charge electric cars. Quite a list.

However, customer participation did not run smoothly. By 1908, Michelin had learned that consumers needed a lot of extra stimuli to participate in such a thing. The company launched a competition. The person to send in the most corrections got 1,500 francs. The rest of the total prize money of 3,500 francs, about 20,000 euros today, would be divided over the seven other finalists.

Nonetheless, the contest showed the Michelin brothers that this form of crowdsourcing was still not a sufficient means of gathering enough information and that it probably never would be. They decided to change course and started focusing more and more on the commercial businesses wanting to be in the Michelin Guide. For example, the hotels would have to engage to offer fixed prices for a fixed supply in order to be included, which lowered the need for corrections by the car drivers.

As we all know, the Michelin Guide became a huge success. Ever since the launch, 30 million copies have been sold. It features information on over forty thousand businesses in three continents.[65]

However, this was not enough for André Michelin, who saw other ways to try and get drivers to cross longer distances.

The South of France became a popular location for wealthy Parisians. Michelin was starting to sense that the information in the guide was not specific enough for these kinds of individual trips. André knew he could do better.

In 1907, Michelin opened a 'touristic service', entirely revolving around their guide. It featured detailed maps and looks at stereoscopic pictures of each route, to help get a feel of what to expect. However, this service was especially focused on setting up personal routes. If you wanted to go from Paris to Toulouse, Michelin would tell you in detail what the best route was. If you could not get to the nearest office, you could just ask for our route by mail. Just a couple of days later, and it would already arrive.

Michelin saw this offer as a good way to get to know their consumers. As a kind of personalized CRM *avant la lettre*. The company also grabbed every opportunity it saw to point out the quality and the speed of their service. André repeatedly recounted the story of a driver asking for a route by letter. He wanted to start in Paris and travel to the Rhine-valley, the Black Forest, Munich, Innsbruck and Tirol, then return via Mount Cenis. The next day, the company had a ninety-page long document for the man. An impressive feat, considering the times, at least according to André. Consequently, the service turned out to be a success: in 1920, 11,200 personal routes were calculated, a number that doubled to 24,300 in 1922 and was up to 155,000 by 1925.[66] Today, the service is called ViaMichelin and is accessible online.

AUGUST OETKER

In turn-of-the-century Germany, another man considered content to be an important element of his marketing efforts. He came up with an idea that is still used today as well. Meet August Oetker.

How Dr. Oetker used recipes for inspiration (Source: Dr. Oetker)

In 1891, he took over a pharmacy in the German city of Bielefeld. He added a laboratory to run several experiments. One of the products he invented was foot cream. Another product he experimented with was baking powder. As his dad was a baker, he knew how difficult it was to make bread airy.

So, in 1891, he launched the baking powder under the name Backin.[67] He did not invent baking powder but found a way to make one that makes every cake rise. Each and every time, which could not be said about other baking powders. We can imagine there was a lot of interest in the powder. It became a success, because it did make baking way easier and produced better results.

Backin was a new product. August understood that he needed to tell women what they could do with it, other than baking bread or cake. So, he started printing recipes on the back of the bags. Not long after, he published his first cook book. It seemed to be the right idea, it stood the test of time. To this day, Dr. Oetker publishes recipes, digital and printed.

Content marketing was anything but limited to Europe, though. Across the pond, a couple of other brands were laying the foundation of this marketing strategy as well. There were brands like John Deere, manufacturer of agricultural machines.

JOHN DEERE

John Deere, founder of Deere & Company, went down in history as 'the inventor of the plow that broke the plains'.[68] In 1836, he was working as a blacksmith in the American state of Illinois. Deere's customers were farmers and cowboys, attracted to the wide prairies of the Midwest, the land stretching out from Minnesota to Ohio. This was the promised land for many 19th century pioneers.

They often asked him to fix their ploughs, the cast iron was no match for the heavy and sticky prairie soil.[69] Deere was convinced that a polished steel plough would do a better job. He developed such a plough in 1837 and brought it to market. It immediately became a commercial success. His company was born and grew to become the world player it is today.

His son, Charles Deere, started working at the company as an accountant. Five years later, in 1854, his father asked him to run the company. The then twenty-year-old had a flair for sales and marketing his father lacked. In 1895, Charles had *The Furrow* printed for the very first time, a three-monthly magazine for farmers.[70] For the first couple of years it was merely an advertorial. From 1901 onwards, it became an actual magazine, paying less attention to the specific John Deere products it wanted to promote. 'How to make your farming company profitable?' became the main theme. 'How to get more out of your harvest?' 'What is the best way to work with labourers?' Apparently, a lot of farmers took an interest: in 1912, the magazine reached over 4 million American readers.[71]

The Furrow still exists, it has a website and can be found on Facebook and Twitter as well. The printed version is distributed in twelve languages and read in 115 countries.[72] It is the biggest agricultural magazine in the world. What the *Rolling Stone* is for the music lover, that is what *The Furrow* is for the farmer.

The cover of the second edition of *The Furrow* from 1897 (Source: John Deere)

The Michelin Guide, Dr. Oetker's cook books, John Deere's *The Furrow*: they are all examples of excellent content marketing that has stood the test of time. A brand walking in the footsteps of these giants is the energy drink Red Bull. Red Bull Media House is a multi-platform media company with a focus on sports, culture and lifestyle. It manages fifteen publications: from digital content to magazines, movies and TV-content. Red Bull's Facebook page has over 46 million followers, the YouTube-channel has collected over a billion views. The brand sponsers over six hundred athletes, has three Formula One teams and five football teams. It is a worthy successor to the content market-eers from the previous century.

WILLIAM WRIGLEY

In the US, there was another entrepreneur who used marketing in just as innovative a way as André Michelin: William Wrigley Jr.

In 1891, Wrigley was selling his father's soap. He wants sales to go up but does not really know how to go about it. One day, he wonders whether he could reward his dealers if they buy more soap than originally planned. Maybe they would do so if they got something in return, an umbrella maybe? It works. The sales incentive is born. Sometimes it is umbrellas, other times it is bags of baking powder or cookery books. Wrigley even adds gum to the mix. However, he notices that the candy is more popular than the actual soap. Way more popular. To the extent that he even considers letting go of his father's soap business to start his own company, a bubble gum company.[73]

In 1893, he launches two types of bubble gum, Wrigley's Spearmint and Wrigley's Juicy Fruits, both still for sale. He used the same sales mechanism as with his father, though he offered more expensive incentives, like shopping tills. The sales went up, but not in the same way the soap did. Gum was a product with slim margins and the tills were putting a lot of pressure on his revenue. He was making a loss. There had to be another way, maybe he had to focus less on the merchants and more on the customers. Though that was easier said than done: his gum did not even come close to the 'classic' status it has today. He needed to find a way to reach and convince the American consumer with one fell swoop.

There is a reason why the man went down in history as one of the most innovative marketeers of his time. In 1915, he did something entirely unprecedented. He send a pack of gum to every American registered in the phone book. He assumed that, if they could afford a telephone, they could afford a pack of gum. One and a half million people got four bars of gum in the mail. It was the first direct marketing campaign ever and it launched Wrigley straight into the (phone-owning) hearts of Americans, never to be let go again.[74]

ALLAN ODELL

Clinton Odell was looking for a success product. The Burma-Vita Company, which he founded with his two sons, was going through a rough patch. He decided to try selling shaving cream. There was already such a product on the market, the English Lloyd's Auxesis, but it lacked quality. Odell thought he could do better. He launched Burma Shave in 1925, but the consumers were not very impressed. He maintained his faith in the product though and started to look for a way to increase the demand for it, however, his money was running out fast.

An example of a Burma-Shave verse (Source: Wikipedia)

Allan, one of his sons, had an idea: he wanted to put wooden boards at the side of the road, six next to each other, like gas stations announcing that travellers can fill up, change oil, eat and go to the bathroom. Every one of these messages on a different plaque.[75] Allan wanted a couple of those next to each other with a rhyme written on them. 'It will work', he told his father. The roads were wide, cars could only drive 30 miles an hour and there were no message boards for miles to see. Even though they were small, they would not be overlooked. His father was not convinced but nonetheless gave him two hundred dollars to test the idea.

Allan placed a couple of signs along the route to Albert Lea and Red Wing, close to the Burma-Vita Company. He was hoping that the drivers would read the signs and look for the product in the stores. 'Shave the modern way / No brush / No lather / No Rub-in / Big tube 35 cents drug stores / Burma Shaves.', that is what drivers read on the road. It worked: at the end of 1925, the company reached a turnover of 68,000 dollars. A serious improvement, as he barely broke even before. The year after, returns had increased to 135,000 dollars.[76] The company made more signs and placed them next to more roads. The messages became more and more humorous: 'Every shaver/Now can snore/

Six minutes more/Than before/By Using/Burma Shave.' They became more confident in this form of communication.

At their peak, the Burma-Vita Company placed seven thousand signs in forty-five states. Not all of the rhymes were made by the company themselves, they held a yearly competition. Everyone could send in their rhymes, the best ones were rewarded with a hundred dollars. Some years the company got over fifty thousand entries.

The verses evolved into public service announcements. Sometimes it was about road safety:

'Past schoolhouses / Take it slow / Let the little / Shavers grow / Burma-Shave',
or:
'Is he lonesome / Or just blind / This guy who / Drives / So close behind? / Burma-Shave'

The company made over six hundred rhymes in total. All friendly, humorous and open-minded. For drivers, they broke up the monotonous roads and children could read them out loud from the back seat.[77] They were often cited and commented upon in radio shows. They became a part of American culture.

All of it ended in 1963, for two reasons. First the government regulated advertising boards alongside the roads: big boards, like we still know today, are allowed, but smaller signs such as Burma-Shaves' were prohibited. Secondly, the company was sold to tobacco producer Phillip Morris. Of course, they did not want to take any risks and got rid of the signs following their attorney's advice.

The last rhyme was:

'Our fortune / Is your / Shaven face / It's our best / Advertising space / Burma-Shave'[78]

In 1999, the Burma-Shave campaign was nominated by Ad Age as one of the best of the 20th century. For one because the advertiser managed to make their campaign a part of popular culture. People were talking about it, making their own versions even, but also, because they had invented their own marketing technique. Some even claim it to be the first application of what is now known as guerrilla advertising.

In 1920, forty-six-year-old American psychologist Edward L. Thorndike conducted an experiment. He asked two officers to evaluate their soldiers based on a couple of factors: intelligence, appearance, leadership qualities and personality traits. Thorndike wanted to know whether a high score on one factor influenced the others. The answer was positive. Especially that appearance had a strong correlation with the other qualities. In other words, the better a soldier looked, the more he was seen as a leader or as someone with a strong personality.[79] The psychologist called it the halo effect: the presence of a certain quality suggests that other qualities are present as well.

Marketeers understood the value of this effect. They started paying stars to link themselves to their brands. Celebrity endorsement was born.

On the 19th of January 1953, Lucy Ricardo gave birth to a son, Little Ricky. 46 million Americans experienced it with her on TV. In other words: over seven out of ten families owning a television were glued to the screen.[80] Eisenhower's inauguration the day after only gathers 15 million more Americans. Radio journalist Walter Winchell said in his show on Sunday: 'This was a banner week. The nation got a man and Lucy got a boy.'[81]

Lucy Ricardo was a fictional character, the main character of the sitcom *I Love Lucy*. Not just any sitcom: one of the most popular American sitcoms ever made, topped only by *Seinfeld* a couple of decades later. The telephone agencies knew exactly when *I Love Lucy* started on a typical Monday evening: the telephone traffic almost died out completely. The New York taxi drivers took a break on Monday evening to watch the show in their favorite bar. In Chicago, there was a warehouse with a sign at the door: 'We love Lucy too. So from now on we will be open Thursday night instead of Monday's.'[82] Lucy and her husband Ricky, portrayed by Lucille Ball and her husband Desi Arnaz, were mega stars. People listened to what they had to say, both in real life as in the sitcom.

I Love Lucy was commissioned by Philip Morris and produced by The Biow Agency, one of the top ten American advertising agencies of the '50s. These are the days when advertising agencies are making fully-fledged shows. Milton Biow was the owner of the bureau.

Philip Morris became a client in 1933. Immediately, Biow started looking for new ways to promote the products of the company. He found inspiration in a hotel. If you had to look for someone in a hotel lobby in the '30s, you would not do it yourself, but call a bellboy to run around the lobby calling: 'Call for Mister ...' Considering Philip Morris was the name of a person, it seemed like an interesting idea to work with and see what it could do.

Biow needed a bellboy, preferably one with a good voice. He went to the Commodore Hotel in New York and asked around for the best bellboy in town. That was Johnny Roventini, who worked in the New Yorker Hotel. Biow immediately went to the hotel, gave the young man a dollar and asked him to find one Philip Morris. Roventini ran about the hotel, calling for Philip Morris. Later he would say: 'I went around the lobby yelling my head off, but Philip Morris did not answer my call.'[83] Back then, he was not yet aware that his 'Call for Philip Morris' would be heard on TV and radio for years to come.

Roventini became the first and only 'living trademark'[84] in the history of advertising. He represented Philip Morris for forty years, appearing in papers and magazines, on posters and on the radio.

On the radio, everything went well. So well in fact, that Philip Morris and Biow decided to give Roventini his own radio show: Johnny represents. The show would be on air for twelve years. He even got a second show: Philip Morris Playhouse, that would run for fourteen years. They did also try the last one on TV, but it did not go too well. Radio worked best for Philip Morris, the company was sponsoring over forty shows.[85]

However, radio was not enough for Biow. Television was new and exciting, attracting more and more viewers. He wanted Philip Morris on TV, whatever the cost. In 1951, he saw his shot. A radio star, Lucille Ball, wanted to bring her show to television. Lucille and her husband, Desi Arnaz, the other star of the radio show, made a pilot. They called it 'I Love Lucy'. Biow was one of the first to see the pilot episode. He did not hesitate and bought the show to offer it to Philip Morris. He then went to NBC and CBS. With Philip Morris on his side, he let them fight for the show, with CBS coming out on top. It offered its best time slot: Monday evening at nine p.m. Prime-time could not get any better. Quite the accomplishment for a show that had never been aired on TV.

What Philip Morris did with I Love Lucy, we cannot imagine today. Most episodes started with the 'Call for Philip Morris' by Roventini. Meanwhile people were constantly smoking and throwing phrases about like: 'Do not say cigarette. Say Philip Morris.' The commercials were immersed into the show, so much so, you could never really tell whether Lucy and Ricky were advertising something or actually playing a scene. They were basically live commercials, and it did not stop there: a whole episode would later be devoted to the making of a Philip Morris commercial.[86]

Today a show influenced by marketeers to this extent would not get any viewers at all. Back then, it was completely normal. Every marketeer wanted a star in their show, they all knew what Thorndike's halo effect could mean for their products and the stars were easily convinced. After all, they knew that marketeers could make shows big, and thus the actors in them as well. Ball and Arnaz are not the only stars marketeers were backing. Comedian Groucho Marx worked for De Soto, the car brand. Frank Sinatra was siding with Timex and Colgate Shampoo.

Marketeers even took it one step further. They wanted to engage the stars outside of their working hours. They wanted to involve them into merchandising, marketing campaigns and promotions. They even wanted to use them for opening new factories or for fundraisers by the boss' wife.[87] The public adored it. A Hollywood celebrity coming to the factory, there was no getting closer to the unattainable stars than that.

Towards the end of the '50s, the hegemony of the marketeers over the shows came to an end. Scandals came to light regarding a couple of popular quiz shows. Networks wanted more and more decision-making power when it came to programming and marketeers were kept out of the shows and got banned to the commercial breaks.

However, companies like Procter & Gamble lasted. It is their radio shows we started calling soap operas in the '30s and they made quite a lot of them. Twenty in total, first on radio and later expanding to TV. Some of those shows kept going for a surprisingly long time. *Guiding Light* ended in September 2009, after being on air for 72 years. *As The World Turns* lasted 54 years, with the last episode airing on the 17th of September 2010.[88]

BILL BERNBACH

The '50s are synonymous with economic growth. World War II is over, the world is being rebuilt. Jobs are in abundance, the general spending power is increasing.[89] We are becoming consumers, buying things because we want them, not because we need them. Or to show how well off we are. Status is becoming an important motive.

These were the years of the 'Big Corporations', ran with a steady hand, following a stern hierarchy, which was also reflected in advertising. Advertisements were not talking about what the consumer needed, but about what a company sold.[90] 'Listen to us, we know what is good for you and what you need to buy'. Adverts needed to follow the rules, follow the formula. Everything was based on standard techniques. There was no room for intuition or something out of the box.

Bill Bernach grew sick of it. He was 36 years old and worked for Grey Advertising in New York. He wrote the management a memo that would go down in history as the start of a creative revolution in our industry.

'There are a lot of great technicians in advertising. And unfortunately, they talk the best game. They know all the rules. They can tell you that people in an ad will get you greater readership. They can tell you that a sentence should be this short or that long. They can tell you that body copy should be broken up for easier reading. They can give you fact after fact after fact. They are the scientists of advertising. However, there is one little rub. Advertising is fundamentally persuasion and persuasion happens to be not a science, but an art. Let us blaze new trails. Let us prove to the world that good taste, good art, and good writing can be good selling.'[91]

The legendary 1947 letter of Bill Bernbach (Source: Digiday UK)

The management put the memo aside. Bernbach responded accordingly and left the company to start his own agency Doyle Dane Bernbach. DDB, headed by Bernbach, handled advertising differently. His new way of working still inspires marketeers today.

Firstly, he wanted a nonnegotiable respect for the intelligence of the consumer. 'Do not treat them like infants who need to be told something repeatedly before they remember. Include the consumer into the story. And yes, sometimes he has to read between the lines to get the message. It makes it more interesting and guarantees he will at least remember the advert.'

Secondly, he questioned the 'hammer it in' principle: 'We can say the right thing about a product and nobody will listen. We have got to say it in such a way that people will feel it in their gut. Because if they do not feel it, nothing will happen.'[92] Time and time again, he proved the power of the emotional connection between a consumer and a brand.

Thirdly, he sided with the truth and despised hollow promises. 'A product advantage does not need to be glorified. It will only disappoint when the product is used for the first time and will result in a growing distrust in adverts to come.'

Finally, he looked for cooperation with the consumer. He understood that campaigns worked better for his clients if he could get the consumers talking about it. The more surprising the campaign, the bigger the chance the consumers would hear and talk about it. He was the first to evaluate the true value of the Watercooler effect, as well as the first to crack the code to activate it.

The best example is a 1969 TV-commercial for Volkswagen. It is the story of a billionaire's funeral. For every marketeer, it seemed like the worst thing you could ever do. This was in no way a story to link to a brand. Yet, DDB did it and it became one of the classics of the VW Think Small campaign.

We see a row of black limousines on their way to a funeral. A voice starts to speak. It is the billionaire's. He starts reading his will:

'To my wife Rose,
who spent money like there was no tomorrow,
I leave 100 dollars and a calendar.
To my sons, Rodney and Victor,
who spent every dime I ever gave them on fancy cars and fast women,
I leave fifty dollars in dimes.

To my business partner, Joules,
whose only motto was spend, spend, spend,
I leave nothing, nothing, nothing.
And to my other friends and relatives who also never learned the value of a dollar, I
leave a dollar.
Finally, to my nephew, Harold,
who ofttimes said: "A penny saved is a penny earned", and who also ofttimes said:
"Gee, Uncle May, it sure pays to own a Volkswagen",
I leave my entire fortune of one hundred billion dollars.'[93]

You can clearly recognise Bernbach's signature here. The commercial is subtle, sensitive and sober. And that is what makes it emotionally touching. The
sympathy you feel for the nephew flows over to the reasonably priced Beetle.
A true piece of high quality advertising.

Another good example of DDB's advertising philosophy is the campaign the
company made for car rental company AVIS. AVIS was the underdog, beating
market leader Hertz by making consumers pick their side. In fact, the campaign worked so well, that Hertz felt the need to respond. This was the very
first time in advertising history this happened.

Finding a gap in the car rental market, Warren Avis, an Air Force officer,
launched AVIS in 1946. While other car rental companies were based in
the cities, he launched AVIS in airports, making it easy for travelling business people to rent a car upon landing.[94] It worked, but not well enough to
dethrone Hertz. In 1962, AVIS had a market share of 11%. Having showed
no profit in the past thirteen years, something needed to be done. Robert
Townsend, then president of AVIS, discussed the situation with the people of
DDB. 'Are your cars newer than Hertz'?', the people of DDB ask. 'Not really'.
'Are you present in more airports?' 'No'. 'Are you cheaper?' 'No'. 'Is there any
difference between you both?' 'Yes', Townsend says, 'We try harder'.[95] The
campaign idea is born. DDB positions AVIS as the underdog. The company
that does not give up, that keeps fighting. An attitude that resonates with
many Americans as being ultra-American and thus incredibly relatable. This
campaign did what no other campaign had ever done before: it turned AVIS'
number two-position into a strength: we need to work harder, we are only
number two on the market.

The campaign was a hit. Within a year, AVIS grew from a loss of 3.2 million
dollars to a return of 1.2 million dollars. Their market share rose as well: in
1966, the company already had a 36% market share. Hertz's management

could do nothing but watch.[96] AVIS knew so and used it in their campaign, involving consumers in the fight with Hertz and making them choose sides: 'Can you believe we are now number 1.5?' And it worked. Hertz knew they needed to respond, so they did, literally: 'For years, AVIS has been telling you Hertz is No. 1. Now we are going to tell you why', headed a full page advert. AVIS' answer does not take long: 'Why No. 1 has to do something about AVIS'. It was one of the most iconic fights ever to be conducted through advertising. It only stopped in 2012, when AVIS dropped their 'We try harder' baseline.

The 'We try harder' campaign from Avis (Source: Google Images)

David Ogilvy called the AVIS campaign an example of 'diabolic positioning'.[97] It looked for one of the opponent's strengths and turned it against him. AVIS was number two and they made it their strength. With the Beetle campaign, DBB did the same. All American cars are big, the Beetle is small and ugly. The campaign worked with this by saying: Think small' and 'It is ugly, but it gets you there'.

Bernbach felt that American culture was changing in the '60s. The 'bigger and better' consumerism was making way for more humility and respect for the consumer. He linked the culture to the brands in such a way that consumers started talking about them. That is the reason why his campaigns quickly became a part of popular American culture.

However, Bill Bernbach is not the only Mad Man from the period of the creative revolution, there are also David Ogilvy and Leo Burnett. These men are seen as the 'Big Three'.[98] Which one of the three can be considered the greatest, is up for debate. For me, it is Bill Bernbach who changed our thinking and our work the most. His signature can still be recognized today.

THERE IS NO NEED TO REINVENT THE WHEEL

The 20th century was a busy time for our industry, with plenty of innovation. In the first half of the century a lot of new advertising techniques were introduced. We are still applying them today, most of them in a digital alternative. In the second half of the century, we worked on the language we use. We went from screaming to subtle, from loud to modest, from very serious to moderately humorous. We learned to respect the opinion of the consumer and we learned to appreciate the effect of consumers putting their efforts behind a campaign.

The giants of our industry taught us valuable lessons–lessons that are still very relevant, as we shall see in the next chapter.

CHAPTER 4

THE NEGATIVE IMPACT OF SHORT-TERM THINKING

'TACTICS WITHOUT STRATEGY IS THE NOISE BEFORE DEFEAT. STRATEGY WITHOUT TACTICS IS THE SLOWEST ROUTE TO VICTORY.'

SUN TZU

We believe we are rational creatures who base their decisions on objective facts. We know that emotions come into play sometimes, but we mostly seem to be able to control them. Or so we believe.

In 2011, Nobel Prize winner in Economic Sciences Daniel Kahneman swept these thoughts off the table. In his research he concluded that our emotions control our decision making 90% of the time without us even being aware of it. At the same time, Kahneman provided a scientific basis for what the giants of marketing intuitively felt in the past: we have to influence the heart, much more than the head. We have to focus on people's emotions, make them laugh, or cry. Convincing consumers to buy products based on rational arguments, seems to be way more difficult.

Kahneman showed that our brain works in two ways. He called it System 1 and System 2 thinking. System 1 is our Auto-pilot, it is on the whole day. System 2 is the Lazy Thinker, also on the whole day, but it leaves most decisions to System 1. System 2 does get constant input from System 1: impressions, emotions and impulses. It takes everything in. If certain impressions and emotions recur often enough, System 2 will turn them into a conviction. The same goes for impulses. If they recur often enough, they will turn into behavior, become certainties, part of your mental construct. System 2 lets System 1 know that it is alright not to reflect upon it. It basically says: if this happens again, you know what to do, you do not need me anymore. Each part of the mental construct falls under the automatic decision making process of System 1. System 2 will only jump in if the automatic pilot does not know what to do with the information it is receiving, because it does not corroborate with the existing framework. That is how System 1 builds on emotion, System 2 on ratio.

If someone frowns their eyebrows during a conversation, we intuitively know that something is wrong. Our autopilot knows that we frown when we do not understand or agree with something. It lets us know something is up, we recognize the emotion. We feel how the other person is feeling without even having to think about it for a millisecond, our intuition does so for us.

When we read this,

234 x 45 = ?

our automatic pilot cannot help us. We will have to think rationally about this. It will take our brain some time to make the calculations. Our autopilot will not do and lets System 2 know it needs help. The Thinker will shift into action.

Another example is learning how to drive. In the beginning it is not easy, it is actually quite tiring. That is because we are putting our System 2 into over-drive. We have to think of everything at the same time. Shifting into neutral before we start, slowly pushing on the gas pedal. Avoid the car jolting. Stop before we take a right. Make sure to use our indicator lights. It is an onslaught of rational considerations. We are exhausted when we step out of the car, because, after all, System 2 requires a lot of energy.

After a couple of months, however, this is a fully automated process and we are ready to listen to the radio or day-dream for a second while driving. Everything is on autopilot, until we pass a cyclist and notice a potentially dangerous situation. In a millisecond we switch over to System 2 and give the situation our utmost attention.

The Autopilot	The Lazy Thinker
Fast	Slow
Unconscious	Conscious
Automatic	Effortful
Everyday decisions	Complex decisions
Error prone[99]	Reliable

From Kahneman's research we can conclude that 90% of our decisions are made on autopilot. However, they are not always the right decisions. For example, let us solve this simple puzzle:[100]

'A bat and a ball together cost 1.10 euros.
The bat costs one euro more than the ball does.
How much does the ball cost?'

Most of us will probably answer 10 cents, but that is not correct. If the ball costs 10 cents, then the bat would cost 1.10 euros and the total would amount to 1.20. The ball only costs 5 cents. What happened here? The auto pilot offered us an immediate answer. Intuitively System 2 did not intervene, because it did not see a reason to do so, as for System 1 the answer was obvious. However, if we hesitated for a moment, because we had an inkling that this was going to be a trick question, then System 2 would have jumped into action. In the absence of doubt, our intuition takes charge.

Why? Because System 2 is inherently lazy. It tries to do as little as possible in order to conserve energy. Kahneman phrased it as follows: 'Thinking is to humans as swimming is to cats; they can do it but prefer not to.'[101] So, we have an Automatic Pilot and a Lazy Thinker.

WHAT CAN WE TAKE AWAY FROM THIS?

If we want sustainable growth, we will have to make sure that our brand ends up in the mental framework of the consumer. If choosing our brand becomes pure intuition, the consumer will not even think before they take our product out of a row of alternatives on the shelf. Once we succeed, it will take a lot for the Automatic Pilot to wake up the Lazy Thinker again.

Consumers build their mental constructs based on emotions and impressions. If these recur often enough, they become a reflex. So, we will have to touch our consumers emotionally and repeatedly if we want them to build a branded mental house in their brains.

However, if we want to temporarily stimulate our sales against competing brands, we will have to put the Lazy Thinker to work. We will have to confuse the Automatic Pilot with something that grabs the attention, something surprising that does not fit into the usual norm. Only then will the Lazy Thinker tell the Automatic Pilot that there is a better choice to be made.

'System 1 runs the show, that is the one we want to move', dixit Kahneman.[102] So, it is in all of our interests to get consumers to build mental frameworks around our brands, so that we become a part of those 90% of decisions that people make based on their Automatic Pilots. The giants of advertising felt this intuitively and showed us how successful we can be when we do so.

However, when we look at advertising today, it is obvious that we are doing the complete opposite. We are focused on the Lazy Thinker. We try to convince the consumers with rational arguments. Campaigns that focus on emotions are far and few between.

We do this because we are focusing on the short-term. Our attention is set on the next quarter. Our campaigns are not made to work on a long-term basis, but to get results tomorrow. It seems we are unconsciously deciding to block the Automatic Pilot. And we have been doing so for ten years. Only: is this beneficial to our brand? Have we forgotten the teachings of the giants?

THE PERFECT STORM OF THE SHORT-TERM-ISM

In 2008 the financial crisis hit, going down in history as the worst crisis since the 1930s. We quickly learned to be scarce. The budgets got smaller. What was left was to be spent on short-term actions. The long-term became less and less important, the CEO lived from quarter to quarter, as did the Chief Marketing Officer (CMO). We got angry looks whenever we asked for a bigger budget to support the brand. Which made sense, as brand building was a luxury problem. Not failing was the more prominent issue. Sales needed to go up, quarter by quarter. We pulled out all the possible rational arguments to convince the consumer to buy our products.

Meanwhile, the rise of the internet was unstoppable, adding ever more screens and platforms. We needed to catch up. We were making websites, mobile websites, mobile apps and brand pages on social media. All with that same smaller budget. And smaller budgets require more efficiency. The procurement departments expanded. Strategic and creative work was out-sourced like toilet paper at Tesco: as much as possible, as cheap as possible.

All digital platforms generate data. Data flows in in real time. Spreadsheets are replaced by dashboards. We follow what is going on as it happens. Some-times a number will turn red, upon which we react immediately. We do not have a choice, we are expected to. After all, we cannot just keep numbers in the red, can we?

Finally, brand guardians – the CMOs and the marketing managers – are hav-ing ever shorter tenures. An American CMO of a top 100 advertiser holds the same job for an average of 42 months.[103] That means 3.5 years. Compared to the average tenure of a CEO (7.2 years) or a CFO (5.6 years) this is very short. CMOs are doomed to work on a short-term basis. They do not get the opportu-nity to work on long-term plans, never mind execute them.

The financial crisis, procurement, smaller budgets, real-time data, the shorter tenures of the brand guardians. It all forced us into a short-term mind-set. Short-term thinking became the new norm. We do not pay any more atten-tion to what is coming after us. Is that a good or a bad thing?

THE PENDULUM MAY HAVE SWUNG
TOO FAR THE OTHER WAY

Consumer companies in the United States are growing at a rate of 2% in 2016. Not that much considering their accumulated advertising budget amounts to 200 billion dollars.[104] Only 241 of the Furtune-500 companies in the US can put forward stable or growing results. In other words: 52% of them are showing negative growth.[105] When we look to the worldwide top hundred advertisers, we can conclude that over half fail to grow. In 2016, 56% of the top one hundred were not growing or were growing negatively.[106] Something is definitely wrong.

More and more voices are calling out the dominance of short-term thinking and the Rational Communication Model attached to it. Mark Ritson, outspoken professor of marketing at MIT Sloan School of Management talks about the 'Spreadsheet Jockeys': 'I increasingly meet these marketeers all over the world. They usually have no marketing training. However, what they lack in formal training, they make up for in technical capability.'[107] This reminds us a little bit of Bill Bernbach's memo from 1947. He then had the same feeling: advertising had become too much of a 'thing for technicians'.

We did and are indeed reverting to the advertising mind-set from before the creative evolution. In our quest for immediate results, we are overwhelming consumers with rational arguments. The commercial breaks are filled with summaries of rational product advantages, one after the other, each thirty seconds long. It is like a catwalk for the mind, with the Lazy Thinkers and the Automatic Pilots as an audience. The Automatic Pilots have dozed off completely, because none of what is shown is of any interest to them. It is the Lazy Thinkers at work here, but they cannot work through everything. It is too much too fast, with nothing really lasting or catching on.

Thanks to Kahneman, we now know this catwalk is a dead end. The more we activate System 2, the more vulnerable we become for our opponents' rational arguments. The less we feed System 1, the more deteriorated our foundations for future sales become.

Research company Enders Analysis phrases it differently: if we work on a short-term basis, we are mostly focusing on the end of the sales funnel. We want to stimulate direct conversion with consumers that are ready for it. For the most part, these are existing consumers. Short-term actions do not allow us to get many new people into our funnels. This is a problem, because if we do not keep filling the funnel, the possibilities to convert will become increasingly scarce, until they dry out altogether. The first key to getting new consumers into the funnel, is reach. The larger the reach, the more new consumers we will be able to touch. The second key is emotion. We want to create mental frameworks for our brands. We want to make sure that new consumers start preferring our brand, otherwise we will never get them into our funnel. This means focusing on System 1. In other words: brand building.

According to Enders Analysis, 61% of our campaigns in 2000 were focused on the long-term, 39% on short-term. This coincides nicely with the 60/40 rule, whose importance was reaffirmed. In 2016, the relation had shifted to 49% on a long-term and 51% on a short-term basis. In sixteen years, the share of short-term campaigns rose from 39% to 51%.[108] In the UK, the ratio has grown even more to the advantage of short-term campaigns: 'The proportion of campaigns with activation objectives rose from 47% prior to the global financial crisis to 55% subsequently, but over the four years to 2016 has reached 72% of cases.'[109]

This is not helping and we know it. We are not creating the sustainable growth we need. The pendulum has swung too far and we now have the data to prove it.

OUR SHORT-TERM THINKING IS LOWERING THE EFFECTIVENESS OF OUR CAMPAIGNS

Field and Binet are two respected marketing experts from the UK that dove into the IPA databank. The IPA is the Institute of Practitioners in Advertising, the most important association in the advertising industry. The database contains over a thousand case studies from all over the world, ranging from 1998 up until now. It is the world's largest database of advertising campaigns and contains a tremendous amount of data on their results. Have sales gone up? Did the returns increase? Did the brands become more relevant? In other words: lots of information concerning the effectiveness of our campaigns.

Field and Binet trotted through the database, looking for the answer to whether the short-term thinking of the past ten years has made our campaigns more or less efficient. How do they measure the efficacy of a campaign? They measured the commercial impact based on the evolution of certain parameters: revenue, sales, market share, penetration, loyalty and price efficiency. Aside from these, they also measured the effect on brand building. Did the campaign strengthen the brand or not? To do so, they took into account other variables: brand recognition, image, differentiation, fame, commitment, trust and appreciation. The results of all of the variables were then brought together to get a total score of impact.

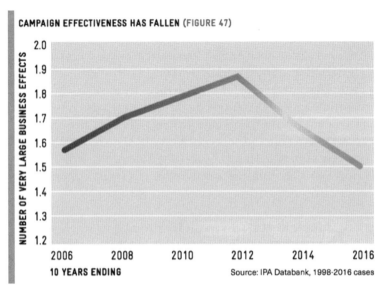

Campaign effectiveness has fallen (Source: Media in Focus)

What does it teach us? The average effectiveness of campaigns has been free-falling ever since 2012. We think it is to our advantage to focus on short-term results. The results however show that the complete opposite is true. An overflow of campaigns aimed at short-term activation is lowering their effect on the most important commercial parameters. The effectiveness of our advertising efforts is decreasing, not increasing. Which of course is not the point of advertising at all.

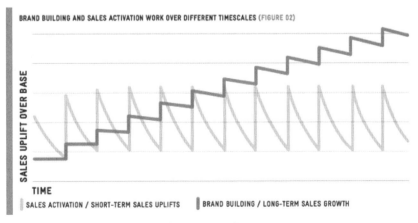

The effect of long- and short-term on sales (Source: Media in Focus)

This evolution leads to a vicious circle. The less efficient our advertising efforts become, the more we are inclined to set up short-term activation campaigns. After all, they bring us immediate, tangible results. However, these effects are only temporary and when they have worn off, we need to set up new actions and continue the cycle.

Obviously, that is not sustainable. As Field and Binet showed, short-term thinking is only resulting in short-lived peaks. Long-term campaigns work on future growth. The time needed for a long-term investment to pay off is, on average, two trimesters. In the current financial context, where we are working from quarter to quarter, working on a long-term basis alone is not an option. Sustainable growth can only be achieved by combining short-term activation with long-term brand building. Short-term and long-term thinking have to come together. Choosing one over the other just is just not a viable option.

In Kahneman's words: we need to activate the Lazy Thinker every once in a while, to achieve a short and powerful peak in sales, but it should not be detrimental to feeding the Automatic Pilot. After all, we want the latter to work the whole time and make the consumer pick our product 90% of the time. That is the best warranty for growth numbers that continue past the short-term peaks into the following years.

Also, we want to make sure the consumer's Automatic Pilot stands strong when our competitor tries to wake up the Lazy Thinker. As we have seen, that one only wakes up when the Automatic Pilot is faced with information outside of its mental frameworks, information that causes doubt. Chances of this happening should be as slim as possible. So, there is only one thing to do: find that right balance, in order to make your campaigns more effective.

WHAT IS THE RIGHT BALANCE BETWEEN SHORT-TERM AND LONG-TERM?

The debate about this question quickly devolves to whether or not we believe or accept theoretical or philosophical models. Let us instead look at the data again. Let us look at the campaigns that have achieved the best results, to see how they succeed in doing so. How much was invested in short-term peaks and how much in long-term growth? When we go back in time and evaluate campaign after campaign up until today, it should give us a good idea about the right share.

What can we conclude? A 60/40 division yields the highest impact. Or to be more exact: 62/38.[110] 62% of yearly investments are best left to strengthening the brand, to feeding the Automatic Pilot. 38% should go to achieving short and powerful sales peaks by activating the Lazy Thinker.

However, these are results based on current and past campaigns. Meanwhile we are living in the digital age. Has the 60/40 ratio survived the digital revolution, or has it changed? Let us take a closer look at the results of the 2016 campaigns.

2016 campaigns with highest impact on:	Brand	Activation
Growth market share	62%	38%
Brand building	58%	42%
Growth revenue	64%	36%
Share of Voice efficiency	64%	36%

Source: Media in Focus (Binet & Field, 2017)[111]

If we look at the campaigns that resulted in bigger market shares, we can see a ratio of 62% for brand building and 38% for activation. If we select the campaigns with the biggest effect on revenue growth, we find a ratio of 64/36. Campaigns with the biggest impact on brand building parameters (image, brand knowledge, differentiation, …) show a split of 58% for brand building as opposed to 42% for activation. If we, lastly, select the campaigns with the biggest effect on the financial returns, then the ratio is 64/36, just like the campaigns with the biggest impact on the growth in revenue.

So, the 60/40 ratio still stands, even in a world running on a new operating system.

WHY WE WANT TO QUICKLY REBALANCE THE SCALE

It is clear that we, because of our short-term focus, have lost precious time. It is important that we are aware of this, because there are two big, uncontrollable changes hurtling towards us marketeers. In order to be sufficiently armed for these changes, we need to fulfill one condition: our brands need to be robust. Difficult times lie ahead for weak brands.

Yet, because of our perpetual focus on short-term results, our brands have become just that: weak. As the IPA data shows as well, the impact on brand building was stagnating ever since 2008, only to start decreasing after 2012.

The first important change is the next step in the technological adoption. We are relying more and more on our technology or algorithms. An algorithm filters the consumer's world, helping him to choose. Or in other words: it wants to make sure buyers will have to make as few choices as possible. How do we make sure that, in a world with an increasing number of filters, our consumers keep choosing our brand, even though filters are suggesting a different one?

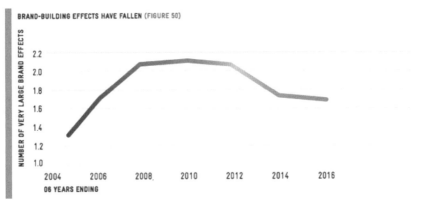

Brand-building effects have fallen (Source: Media in Focus)

The second important change is the upcoming generation switch. Generation Z does not think the same way previous generations did: they are the first generation to have never known a world without Google or Facebook. Compared to other generations, they have different expectations when it comes to brands. And generation Z is used to receiving suggestions from algorithms and responding to filters.

ALGORITHMS ARE AT PLAY

Amazon, Spotify and Netflix. They are companies that want to make customer's lives easier. In order to do so, they use algorithms. They filter their huge supply and wish to do so as precisely as possible. Based on what clients have bought, what they are looking for and what they listen to or watch. Their goal is to eliminate the need to search for things. To have their filters trusted blindly. Their strategy is working: 80% of the films or series watched on Netflix, have been suggested by algorithms.[112] Imagine swiping through that enormous database: impossible.

A lot of algorithms are being put to work already, even without consumers being aware of them. Algorithms determine who they talk to: social media algorithms decide what posts they see. If they do not see anything from certain friends anymore, this does not mean their friends are not posting anymore, the algorithm is just not letting them pop up in their feeds. Out of sight, out of mind: the algorithm has a huge influence here.

Algorithms also decide what customers buy. Amazon's 'Consumers who bought this item also bought...', is quite a familiar one. Today all e-commerce websites have their own algorithms suggesting certain products and leaving others under the radar. And not quite innocently at that. In June 2017, Google was sentenced by the European Union to paying a fine of over 2 billion dollars because the company was caught manipulating their shopping service to negatively impact other websites for price comparisons.[113]

Algorithms influence driving. Once someone has used the navigation app Waze for example, they cannot quite stop. Even early GPSes told users which roads to take, but Waze's algorithm also points out where the speed cameras are, makes sure you do not end up in traffic and lets others follow up on where someone is. Cameras and sensors in cars make sure you keep enough distance between you and the car in front. Or make sure that you drive slower when it rains or when going round a bend. These same algorithms even know at all times whether or not one is following speed regulations.

The algorithms in the Tinder app help you choose who to go to bed with or who to start a relationship with. Algorithms are everywhere and are always ready to filter the world, to help get a handle on a choices overload. This is influencing consumer's brains. Research by Daniel Wegner, a psychology professor at Harvard University, points out that algorithms have become a part of what he calls the 'transactional memory'.[114] This has to do with the way our memory saves data. Ever since the smartphone for example, no one knows phone numbers by heart anymore. Everybody counts on smartphones to do that for them, and as of late on Siri or Alexa. The same happens when driving with a GPS. Most people neglect to remember routes, because they do not need to anymore. They know they can count on the GPS next time as well. People's brains are great friends with Google too. Ever since the search engine came around, they need to remember way less than before. Spotify even takes away the need to remember any album titles, the name of the artist suffices.

Our brain seems to delegate quite a bit to algorithms. Even to the extent that we, according to Wegner, are remembering different things than we did in the past. Like where to find something, instead of what it actually was. Think about how difficult our lives would be, if someone were to pull the plug on the algorithms.

The influence of algorithms goes deeper still. The data smartphones, computers, tablets and smart-watches are collecting is being interpreted by algorithms. They search for what people like so that they can suggest other entertaining things. They learn from shopping behaviour, so that they can suggest products that customers are highly likely to want to buy as well. From browsing and search histories they learn what inspires people, to try and offer them even more and bigger sources of inspiration.

Algorithms are trying to make lives as easy as possible, not because of a sudden urge to do good. They want to become crucial, because the more crucial they are, the easier it is going to be for the companies behind them to build revenue streams on top of them.

TIME TO TALK

While people mostly used to talk to these algorithms through keyboards before, they are slowly but surely starting to use their voices more often. People are already talking to Siri and Google on their phones. With new smart speakers like Amazon Echo and Google Home, they are using their voices even more.[115]

And they love it. Over four out of ten Americans use the personal assistants about ten times per month, accounting for 710 million interactions per month. In the UK, it is expected that 40% of households will acquire an Amazon Echo in 2018.[116] According to experts, 2 billion consumers will be using a personal assistant in 2021. To give an idea of the scale: that is how many users Facebook has today. Considering the impact Facebook had and has on consumers, it is easy to understand that this requires our attention.

Smart speakers can be used for just about anything: to set an alarm, play music, order pizza, read the news, switch smart lights on and off... In 10% of the cases, people use them to shop.[117] If we just focus on the use of Amazon Echo, the numbers are a bit higher. Twenty-five per cent are asking Alexa to put a product in their Amazon shopping carts, 20% use Alexa to buy those products.[118] This is good news for Amazon: Amazon Echo users buy, on average, 6% more from Amazon than before they used Echo.[119] On top of this, they are also now spending 10% more on average than before.[120] More great news.

So, about shopping with a personal assistant... Let us check our last grocery list, what did we write down: toilet paper, toothpaste, beer and ice cream. Not Scottex, Oral B, Heineken and Häagen-Dazs. People tend to use the general name of the product, not the brand. So what happens when they read their shopping list to Alexa or Google Home? Do they ask for toilet paper or a brand of toilet paper?

Imagine asking for toilet paper, what could happen? There are a couple of possibilities. The personal assistant could ask you to be more specific and name a brand. Or it looks at past shopping behaviour and asks if the usual brand is ok. Or it suggests the brand with the best reviews at the lowest price. They had it right before, so customers will likely trust their judgement again and agree to the suggestion.

Scot Galloway, founder and chairman of counselling agency L2, thinks that there is a chance customers might become brand agnostic.[121] That they will just follow Alexa's suggestions, assuming she knows better than they do. After all, she has the data and can easily compare prices. As a matter of fact, Amazon does so very often: every couple of minutes it checks if prices are starting to diverge too much from other platforms. If needed, they will immediately be adjusted, no human intervention required. Alexa also knows best about consumer ratings or reviews from people that have bought the product before. If the reviews are positive and the price agreeable, why would shoppers even hesitate? That all sounds a lot like the System-2 thinking of the 'Lazy Thinker', not at all like the 'Automatic Pilot' of System 1.

Of course, this will not happen overnight. Siri, Cortana, OK Google or Alexa are not about to do all our shopping starting tomorrow, but over time, they will increasingly do so. All experts agree: 'Voice is the next big platform.'[122] And the battle for domination is taking place between Amazon, Google, Microsoft and Apple. Voice-activated personal assistants are hidden in phones, smart speakers and, more and more, in cars. It looks like everybody will be able to talk to Siri or Alexa wherever they are. Which is of course the big goal of the tech companies.

How do we handle this for our brands? Not too long ago, we saw that constantly feeding System 2 is not a good thing. Moreover, we are already dealing with a deficit, for which we need to appeal to System 1.

Brands definitely do not want to leave the decision making to the personal assistants. They decide based on hard, rational facts. Alexa turns out to suggest products that are, first and foremost, labeled as 'Amazon Choice'. A product gets this label if it is available through Amazon Prime and has high scores and reviews. The second category products are chosen from is the Amazon 'Best Sellers' lists.[123] After that, Alexa will look at the products most searched for on amazon.com. Alexa does not leave much choice either, only recommending two products per search. Also, the first recommended product will usually remain the first recommended product.[124] These appear to be Alexa's criteria. Other personal assistants follow their own rules, though these are less clear today.

Thus, the question is how to ensure a spot in the lists used by personal assistants. An obvious way is to meet the criteria set by these assistants. We do so by making sure we have good reviews, high scores, low price points, high relevance and retention rates. However, does this suffice? And how many brands score high on all criteria? Would it not be better if consumers asked for our brand directly? It can be done, but that means continuously reinforcing a strong Automatic Pilot position with consumers. Once again, this is why we need to implement the 60/40 rule and focus on sales activation and brand building at the same time.

Who are the main users of these personal assistants? Without a doubt the millennials and Gen Z: over a third of American millennials used one in 2017.[125] This will only increase, as Generation Z will use it abundantly. In the United States 32% of Gen Z youngsters are already talking to their phones, closely followed by their European counterparts with 25%.[126]

GAME ON FOR GEN Z

Generation Z is growing up. After the baby boomers, Generation X and the Millennials, it will be their time to take over the world. They are numerous as well: in 2020, Gen Z will represent 40% of all consumers in Europe.[127]

Generation Z starts after 1996, so they were two years old when Google got online, five when the first iPod became available and twelve when their parents bought their first iPhones. In Gen Z's world, all knowledge literally lies in the palm of one's hand. In their world, one can watch or listen to whatever, whenever. A world where friends are constantly updating them on what they are doing, seeing or hearing. And this is all completely normal, they never knew otherwise. Their generation is the first generation of real world citizens: our world has never felt as small as it does for them.

However, it is a very down to earth generation. We cannot just tell them anything, every fact can, and thus, will be checked. Growing up during the 2008 financial crisis, they have already seen a lot as well. They grew up with the knowledge that not everything works out and that, sometimes, things can go very wrong. They witnessed the Arab Spring, a real revolution the likes of which past generations did not see. They saw the power of people coming together, especially when combined with social media. They grew up during the debates about global warming, debates that evolved from the question of whether or not it actually exists into whether it can be limited to an increase of two degrees. This generation knows that they are going to be the first generation to truly feel the effects of global warming. Moreover, they also know that it is up to their generation to solve the problem, at least if they want to keep their kids from the same fate. Sobering.

All of this influences the way this generation thinks. 'They do not view ethics as having any grey area; to them, things are black and white with no middle ground', according to Skyler Huff, an American marketing expert.[128] They do not beat about the bush, they have an opinion and take a stand, but they also respect the opinions of others. Likewise, they expect the same attitude from brands. Do not beat about the bush, say what you stand for and what you find important. Having an opinion is more important than having the wrong one.

Ben & Jerry's is a good example of a brand that gets this. In the US, it sells better than Haagen-Dazs[129] as the brand has won the hearts of the millennials and Generation Z. Of course this has to do with its quality and taste, but Haagen-Dazs' products are surely up to par as well. The difference lies in Ben & Jerry's ethical conduct: it takes responsibility. The brand takes a stand, on democracy, global warming, LGBTQ+ rights and fair trade. In October 2016, it openly backed the Black Lives Matter movement.[130] Today's youth can relate to that. It is a brand that thinks the way they think: it has an opinion and voices it.

Unilever has another one of those brands that needs to ensure it is the choice of GenZ: Axe. For years, Axe has built on the 'Axe-effect', or how the prettiest girls will throw themselves at men using Axe deodorant. Up until 2009, that got them a growth of 2%.[131] Then the growth started to slow. Axe was losing their connection to adolescent men. It risked becoming the brand of the dorks, of young men that do not really accomplish anything. It was time to set a new course. But how?

Rob Candelino, vice president and general manager of Unilever Hair Care, understands the necessity of change. 'Brands must go beyond the functional and align with consumer values', he stated in business magazine *Forbes*.[132]

Eighty per cent of adolescents thinks it should be a priority to make the world we live in a better and more pleasant place. In doing so, they are firstly looking at the business world, then to the government and only then to themselves, according to Joeri Van Den Bergh, co-founder of market research bureau InSites Consulting.[133] They have seen how governments hesitate and delay when it comes to, for example, global warming. They know that the business world has more financial and other means to really make a difference if they it wanted to.

Candelino sees another difference from the past. Young consumers are well-aware that what the world of marketing offers them, has nothing to do with actual reality. Everyone knows women will not fall at men's knees because they use Axe, that is not the problem. The problem is that these stories do not catch on anymore. Gen Z is looking for no-nonsense, honest and authentic brands that say it as it is in an honest and authentic way. And Candelino sees this trend getting stronger and stronger: 'It is likely that what are considered trends today – more transparency, more informed consumers, more purposeful brands – will become the norm tomorrow.'[134]

What did this mean for Axe? It meant taking a whole new direction. The theme of their new campaign is 'Find your magic', an ode to individual masculinity. It is a call for every young man to find what makes him unique and take that into the fray. Axe's role has been to just being the accompanying gel or smell. It is for the young man to find his own way.

By doing so, Axe touches upon another one of this generation's qualities. They are aware that nothing is going to be handed to them. They realize that the pampered generation before them, the one that thought they could get anything they wanted if they just screamed loud enough, was wrong. They have gone back to the values of the baby boomers, like taking responsibility for their successes and failures. They think highly of strong work ethics, they want to be independent and continue to educate themselves. You could, in a way, call them a little conservative.

That does not mean that they, like the baby boomers, are counting on companies to offer them lifelong careers. This is a generation taking matters into its

own hands and finding its own way, sometimes at a company, sometimes on
its own.

At the same time, they are very open minded on a couple of other matters. For
them, racism is a problem of the past. As world citizens, they cannot understand that people could still have problems with skintone. Their attention
shifts to problems like gender equality, freedom of sexual preference and fem-
inism. It is important to them that anyone can get along with anyone. This is
linked to how small the world has become. Everyone is connected meaning
that if they want to make the world work, everyone has to work together.
Respect for diversity and inclusion is very important to them.

However, not all is peaches and dandelions. Just like every generation, this
one has its problems. Like a huge sleep deficiency.[135] Half of the fifteen to
eighteen year olds have a chronic sleep deficiency, seven out of ten do not get
their needed nine hours of sleep. This, of course, has everything to do with
their internet usage and the accompanying 'FOMO' and 'FOLO', respectively
the fear of missing out and the fear of living offline. If the whole world is a
village, then there is a lot to read, watch, share and like. You can definitely
not get away with not knowing what your friends are getting up to. They
constantly report about their lives on Snapchat or Instagram. Want to see the
effects of FOMO or FOLO in real life? Just turn off the Wi-Fi at home, enjoy the
following ten seconds of quiet (to let the buffer run out) and then watch all
hell break loose.

This leads us to their media use: the definition of a television no longer is
the same as it was for the generations before them. Today, a television is just
another screen like a laptop or a smart phone, something one uses to watch
Netflix-series on. Unless *The Voice*, the World Cup or the Tour de France is on,
then television becomes television as it was twenty years ago.

Radio is no longer a machine either, but an app. A CD or, imagine, a vinyl collection is cute and trendy, but mostly inconvenient when it is possible to just
stream any song that has ever been made. A subscription to the print version
of a newspaper is pure nostalgia, but not very useful. The world is changing
constantly. Why would you wait until the next day to know everything about
what happened an hour ago? A digital subscription seems like the better
choice. Or Twitter. If anything of importance happens, one can follow it live
there. Only, afterwards everyone leaves straight away, because apart from that
hot news flash there is nothing much going on there.

The most tech-savvy generation yet

Gen Z is the most technological generation yet. Digital has little secrets for our youngsters today. They know marketeers are looking to reach them in their digital worlds, but they are also very down to earth about this. They understand the true value of their attention to brands and they are prepared to give it their attention, in return for value. They have too little time to waste on watching meaningless advertisements.[136] Do not expect them to wait until the advert is over. Do not expect them to give the content of a post a second look on their timeline when it has got the 'sponsored' label on top of it. Give them something to learn from. Give them entertainment. Tell them how you can help them, instead of expecting them to help you. And let it all fit on a smart phone screen. Because if you are not there, you do not matter to them. They communicate with each other and the world through that screen.

What we should avoid at all times is interrupting them. They have neither time nor respect for intrusive advertising. After all, this is the first generation having to process this much content. Some have even said they have an attention span shorter than a goldfish's, but luckily this turned out to be a hoax.[137] Nonetheless, how are they processing all of this content? Well, they rely on curators or influencers. On people they trust and whose selections they follow. Or they trust the trending news on social media.[138] If subsequently, they find a topic that interests them, they dive in head first.

The amount of content that is available just cannot be processed by a normal human being anymore. So, it is quite understandable that they do not appreciate being interrupted in their digesting process. You would get annoyed for less. Since they spend most of their time on digital media, digital advertising receives most of their ire. They are mostly hostile towards advertising on search pages, banners and video ads. 56% skip every advertisement, because of too much crap, too much junk.[139] They are also the biggest users of ad blocking software. Surprisingly enough, they are much more positive about advertising on traditional media.[140]

A very down to earth generation is coming. These people who are done with advertising telling them their dirty kitchen tiles can turn squeaky clean with just one swipe. Or that they can do the dishes for the entire neighbourhood with one drop of detergent. Or that they can attract women with nothing but the right deodorant. The only thing we achieve with these commercials is annoying them and making them look away. If we want to talk to them, let us be honest. Then they might listen, if they want to take the time.

So, we must inspire them. Help them take responsibility for their own success. Tell them how we help them make the world cleaner and more honest. Reassure them that we are all working together and not against each other. We can keep wallowing in the madness and continue to speak the same language we do today, but no good will come of it. Skip. Fast forward. Learn from Axe, learn from Ben & Jerry's. They sit well with this generation. Do so fast, because in merely two years, Gen Z will represent 40% of all consumers.

HOW TO REBALANCE THE SCALE ASAP

By focusing on the short-time for the past ten years, our language towards the consumer has become mostly rational. We have mostly been feeding System 2. We have seen that the effectiveness of our campaigns is going down. We see a decrease in their commercial effect and we see a weakening of our brands. At the same time, we see the rise of algorithms, the next platform shift and Gen Z on their way to becoming consumers. What we need to do now is clear: we need to feed System 1 again. We know that our Automatic Pilot makes 90% of our decisions. We need to make sure that our brands make it into that 90% again and we need to make sure that we adhere to a 60/40 balance in our investments.

Increasingly, marketeers are taking on this notion, including Kevin Hochman, Chief Marketing Officer of fast food chain Kentucky Fried Chicken. At the ANA Masters of Marketing Conference in October 2017 he stipulated: 'Build sales overnight and brands over time – we must do both.'[141]

How should we do this, especially in a relatively short time span? Short because we are coping with a deficit today and the two big changes mentioned earlier are racing towards us. Is there a recipe for success that can earn us both short-term sale results as well as build our brands, helping us also secure our sales results for the future?

THE DIFFERENT COMMUNICATION MODELS

'I have learned that people will forget what you said, people will forget what you did, but people will never forget how you made them feel.' This is one of the famous sayings by Maya Angelou, American writer and poet.[142] The giants of advertising knew this already. Time and time again it has been confirmed by advertising research as well. If we succeed in getting our consumers to remember our ads, then it is not what we are telling them that matters, but how we are making them feel.

This has now been confirmed by neuroscientific research as well. Nielsen, an American research bureau focused on consumers, has proven the link between higher sales and adverts triggering highly emotional reactions. To do so, they measured the electroencephalographic activity (EEG) in the brains of consumers. If a consumer showed an above average EEG-score when seeing an advertisement, then this correlated to an average extra sales of 23%.[143]

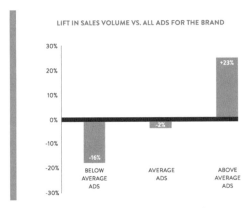

LIFT IN SALES VOLUME VS. ALL ADS FOR THE BRAND

The effect of the EEG-score on sales (Source: Nielsen)

However, let us compare the different communication models, because not all of them focus on emotion.

1. The Rational Communication Model
The classic 'reason why' model. It emphasizes a number of product characteristics and their positive effects. A comparison is made, either explicitly or implicitly, with rival brands or products. No efforts are made to develop an emotional bond with the consumer. Quite the opposite, since the brand tries to appeal to their ratio. A purely sensible argument is put forward. The objective is to reuse, or in the sense of a new product, a first sale. This is the toothpaste or detergent advertising we know from TV, completely focused on feeding System 2.

2. The Rational/Emotional Model
This is the kind of advertisement that first attracts the attention with a piece of rational information, after which an emotional element is introduced to reel the consumer in completely. Or the other way around. The goal is usually to reinforce what the consumer already knows about the product or a brand.

Just about all advertisements from the travelling industry are based on this model. The pretty images in the beginning want to touch you, the price at the end tries to rationally pull you in. Many campaigns from the telecom industry use this model as well, appealing to both System 1 and System 2.

3. The Emotional Communication Model

The objective of this model: to deeply touch the consumer. With a laugh and a tear, it tries to convince the consumer, to build an empathic bond between the consumer and the brand. Because the more empathy, the bigger the influence at the time of sale — at least, that is the reasoning behind it. Making people laugh is difficult, just ask any stand-up comedian. Getting people to cry is even more difficult, as there is a thin line between real and fake tears.

It is equally essential to find the right balance between the importance of the story and the brand. We can tell a fantastic story that the consumer will remember for years to come, but if the same consumer has no clue what the brand was about, we are missing the point. If we do get it right, however, this model works astonishingly well, as we will see later on. It gives System 1 a boost but does not try to affect System 2. So, even though this model will not have its effect on short-term sales results, it will pay off in the long run.

The different communication models

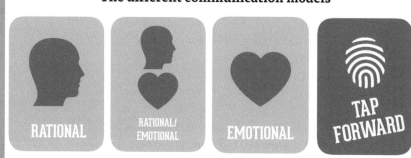

The different communication models

4. TapForward Communcation Model

A laugh and a tear are once again key elements, but with the central objective being to get people talking about the advertisement. The brand wants to trigger a reaction. It wants to make sure that it becomes a conversational topic on the train, on the work floor, over coffee, over a beer, both offline and online. It wants to to do so because of two reasons:

a. **Extra Share of Voice**

The Share of Voice (SOV) is the percentage that a media budget represents compared to the entire market it is active in. In other words: an SOV of 10% stands for a tenth of all media investments in the market. It is important to know the SOV, because data from IPA demonstrates that there is a correlation between the SOV and the Share of Market (SOM). Brands grow if their SOV is bigger than their SOM. So, it is important to have the biggest SOV possible, which is exactly why brands want to implement the TapForward Model. Because, if we manage to get our consumers to respond en masse to our campaign, then that generates extra SOV. If this gets our SOV above our SOM, then we will see our sales numbers go up on our spreadsheets.

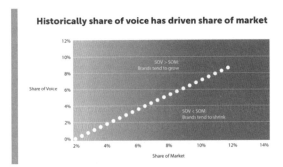

The relationship between Share of Voice and Share of Market (Source: The Long and the Short of It)

b. **Mental availability**

Research points out that brands grow the most by selling to more consumers instead of getting existing consumers to repeat the purchase of a product or a service again (a resell). Intuitively, this seems irrational. The reason, especially in the FMCG category (Fast Moving Consumer Goods) is that most of the consumers are so-called 'light users'. The group of existing consumers will traditionally be smaller than the group that would buy it for the first time. To profit most from this growing opportunity, we have to make sure there is mental availability. This will make consumers, when they go from a 'no buy' to a 'buy', choose our product instead of a rival's. We create mental availability by communicating repeatedly to all consumers, including those that have never bought a product of our brand before. The TapForward effect heightens this availability to multiple people.

How does it differ from the Emotional Model? After all, both of these try to appeal to consumers' emotions. Well, the TapForward Model works in a more inspiring way. It inspires people so much, they share their opinions and the message, both online and offline. The TapForward Model is emotion plus in-spiration, whereas the Emotional Model is limited to emotions. It can inspire as well, but not to the same extent. The TapForward Model works on both System 1 and System 2 at the same time.

To clarify the difference between the emotional and the TapForward Model, we will scrutinize the workings of two worldwide campaigns. One of them is for a brand of whiskey, another one for a telecom company. One followed the emotional model, the other aimed for the TapForward effect.

JOHNNIE WALKER'S
EMOTIONAL COMMUNICATIONAL MODEL

The story of whiskey brand Johnnie Walker starts in 1820. John Walker was a grocer from Kilmarnock, a village in Scotland. In his store, he sold whiskey as well. In those days, distilleries had not yet managed to stabilize the taste of this spirit yet,[144] which differed from bottle to bottle, even if the whiskey came from the same producer. John Walker wanted to solve this problem. He blend-ed (hence blended whiskey) different whiskeys until he managed to produce one with a stable taste. A brand of whiskey was born, one that would grow to take over the world, and is now sold in over 180 countries.

In 1999 countless alarms were going off at Diageo, the mother company of Johnnie Walker. Between 1996 and 1999, sales had gone down by 14%, the market share was in a free fall. Rival companies smelled blood and started to attack the company from all angles. Clearly, sales needed to go up, fast. Not just that, the whole brand needed revamping, it needed to become strong again. A brand with a strong emotional connection with its consumers. A brand with the same perception all over the world. In Europe, Johnnie Walk-er's spot was next to the fireplace. In Latin America it was the foundation of cocktails. In America it was known as the posh whiskey. In Asia it was a status symbol. Thus, the brand needed to make serious work of creating one clear image of the spirit all over the world. However, the people drinking the brand did not all fit into size either. They differed in age, mindset, cultural diversity and economic means. The 27 different campaigns that had been organized to promote the Red and Black Label between 1997 and 1999 had been of no help either. No wonder everyone had a different perception of the brand.

Whiskey brands, just like other alcoholic beverages, represent a lifestyle. They represent certain values. They help consumers define who they are and what they find important. Johnnie Walker needed to find itself, it needed to find its emotional bond with the consumer.

Whiskey has always been slightly linked to masculinity and success. However, what did that mean at the beginning of the 21st century? What did it look like, that masculine success? It seemed that success was no longer linked to having extensive financial means. Success was seen as inner growth, becoming a better person, living a more fulfilling life. Making progress, mentally. This progress could be linked to Johnnie Walker: in 1908, the Striding Man appeared for the first time. It symbolized the entrepreneurship of the Walker family, emitting a certain vitality, a certain vigor. The drawing showed a man who wanted to move on. It became Johnny Walker's Michelin Man, the symbol that appeared in every advert for fifty years. Until it vanished.

The Striding Man (Source: IPA Effectiveness Awards Grand Prix 2008, Warc.com)

The striding man was reintroduced into the campaign of 1999, both visually and intrinsically. In the campaign, famous stars talked about how they had moved up the ranks. How they kept succeeding and exceeding themselves. The Keep Walking Campaign was off to the races.

It was launched with the story of Roberto Baggio, one of the most famous Italian footballers of that time. He is the only player to score in three consecutive world championships for Italy.[145] At the world championship of 1994, he played like a true rock star and took Italy to the final against Brazil. That match ended in a tie. Penalties were needed to determine the victor. Baggio was up last: if he scored, Italy would become world champion. The player was known for his curve balls which were extremely difficult to catch. Baggio took his shot, curving his ball, but a tad too high. The ball shot over the goal. Brazil got the championship title. The Italian footballer kicked himself into history with this failed shot: the shot that made Italy lose the world championship. Until the next championship, four years later.

In 1998, Baggio was at it again. In the quarter final he stood in for Del Piero. Another undecided match, again penalties were to decide the match. Baggio took up the responsibility again. The stadium quieted down. Everyone remembered what had happened four years ago. He ran up and scored. This is how he recounted the tale in the commercial:

'I made a mistake in the 1994 World Cup.
And my country lost.
I missed that penalty every day, for four years.
Four years later, I chose to take another penalty.
How many people watching, believed I could do it?
I'll never know.
What matters is that I believed.
Keep Walking.'

The campaign worked and became a worldwide success. Sales skyrocketed. Johnnie Walker grew faster than expected, year after year.

This was a typical example of employing the Emotional Communication Model. They did not show any product information, they did not say why Johnnie Walker was better than or different from other whiskeys, there were no prices or promotions. There was nothing rational about it: it was purely emotion, working on System 1. The campaign built on the consumer's mental framework. The sympathy created for the main character transferred onto the brand via the halo effect. This all made it more likely for consumers to think of Johnnie Walker, next time they were thinking of whiskey.

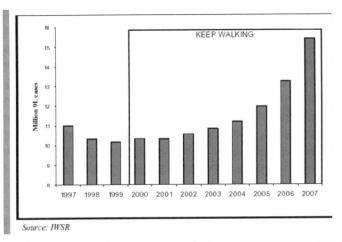

Source: IWSR

The effect of the Keep Walking campaign on sales (Source: IPA Effectiveness Awards Grand Prix 2008, warc.com)

JOHN LEWIS' TAPFORWARD COMMUNICATION MODEL

The TapForward Model builds on emotion but also uses it as a trigger. The goal is to activate the consumer. The model wants them to react, share and comment. It looks for interaction. With consumers, the press, employees and adversaries.

In the UK, competition between stores around Christmas-time is fierce. Supermarkets go all out to get their hands on the Christmas purchases. John Lewis is one of those stores. Its end-of-the year campaign has even become a British tradition. Every year people looked forward to it, and 2015 was no exception. The Daily Telegraph put a countdown on its website, not until the end of the year, but until the 6th of November: the day the John Lewis commercial would be launched.[146] In another paper, speculation even arose as to whether or not Adele would be the singer on the ad.

A week before the launch, the hashtag #ManOnTheMoon was launched on Twitter, with a teaser showing an image of the moon. During the *X-Factor* episode on the 1st of November, the ten second teaser was shown again. On Twitter, there were numerous rumors going around, some suggesting it might be a part of the new John Lewis campaign.

Finally, the day came. At eight o'clock in the morning on the 6th of Noveme-ber the commercial could be seen for the very first time on John Lewis' social media channels. After forty minutes, it hit number one in the World Trending rankings on Twitter. Sixty minutes later, it was mentioned in about 22,429 tweets.[147] Almost 13,000 tweets incorporated the campaign hashtag #ManOn-TheMoon. Only twelve hours later and the advert would appear on TV for the first time.

What did John Lewis say that made people react to this extent, causing such a stir? The commercial told the tale of Lilly, a six-year-old girl. One evening, she was bored and decided to look up at the moon through her telescope. When the moon was in her sight, she saw a shimmer. What could it be? She zoomed in. Another shimmer. She zoomed in even more. As it turned out, there was a house in a crater on the moon. A house with an old man. An old man living in a tiny house. All by himself.

As days went by, Lilly had a look at the moon every night to see the man. He was there. Always. Lonely, he was staring in front of him on the bench next to the house. Lilly racked her brain to find a way to get into contact with the man. She tried and tried and tried. Nothing worked.

On Christmas eve, the man, as always, was sitting on his bench, staring into space. Until he saw a package floating up to him, attached to a couple of Christmas balloons. Lilly found her solution.

The man opened the package and found a telescope. He pointed it at the earth. He found Lilly. And Lilly found him. Finally. A tear dropped from his eye. The ad ended with: 'Show someone they are loved this Christmas'.

It was not just a John Lewis advert, it was the start of the AgeUK movement. AgeUK is an organisation that aids the elderly in society. In cooperation with John Lewis, the organisation wanted to point out that a lot of elderly are lone-ly during the holidays, but that everyone can make a difference. For example, by sending a text to donate five pounds, for which AgeUK made a special version of the ad.

After 24 hours, people had discussed the Man On the Moon commercial 108,000 times on social media.[148] The campaign hashtag was used 55,000 times, 86% of opinions were either neutral or positive.

Christmas sales, year-on-year

	2014	2015
John Lewis	+4.8%	+5.1%
M&S	-5.8%	-5.8%
Debenhams	+2.4%	+1.8%
Argos	+0.1%	-2.2%
Comet	CLOSED	CLOSED
Mothercare	+1.1%	+4.2%

Like-for-like sales, Christmas period (non-food), year on year
Sources: Published financial information

Christmas sales of different department stores in 2014 and 2015 (Source: Les Binet, adam&eve DBB)

The campaign was not just limited to TV or social media. Moon pop-up shops were installed at all eleven stores, accompanied with extra information about the collaboration with AgeUK and a possibility for people to take moon selfies. An augmented reality-app was launched, making the whole thing more interesting by bringing the moon to life.

John Lewis also made a lot of #ManOnTheMoon merchandise, such as calendars, glow in the dark pajamas, the telescope from the commercial, building packages for telescopes, bags, puzzles, pillows, etcetera.[149] A quarter of the sales price went to AgeUK.

However, the campaign was also supported by product communication. The 60/40 rule was applied: 60% went to brand building, 40% to activation, with the activation budget being invested in online video adverts.

In total, the advert was viewed about 1.2 billion times, of which 35 million were online. It was 2015's most searched ad on Shazam. It was mentioned over 1,400 times in the press. It was parodied over five thousand times on the internet as well, the most popular coming from Aldi, earning 2.1 million views. The four most popular parodies reached a total amount of 3.5 million views.

Clearly, the campaign was a huge success. It quickly became the most searched, shared and discussed campaign John Lewis had ever made.

What was the result, business-wise? The week after the launch was the first week of the year in which John Lewis sold over 100 million pounds, a rise of almost 16% compared to the week before the launch.[150] A great start, resulting in high expectations for the rest of the Christmas period.

Expectations were indeed met: John Lewis became the winner of the Christmas period. The department store saw more consumers stepping into their stores, spending more compared to the year before. The retailer beat all of its rivals and ended 2015 with a market share of 29.6%, the highest ever.

The Man On The Moon campaign was a typical TapForward campaign. Everything was set to generate as much interaction as possible among the consumers and the press. Of course, the cherry on top was that a competitor – in this case Aldi – deemed it necessary to step into the debate. It was all a bit reminiscent of the feud between AVIS and Hertz.

THE TAPFORWARD COMMUNICATION MODEL HAS THE HIGHEST MID-TERM BUSINESS EFFECT

Thanks to the TapForward effect a campaign can achieve way more reach. We already saw how this results in higher sales, but is it a sustainable impact? Does the TapForward Model always result in better or higher sales? And does it indeed push other commercial parameters upwards?

What did Field and Binet find in their research? The TapForward campaigns achieve better results on every commercial factor studied.[151] Not only do they positively affect sales results and market share, revenue, penetration and loyalty also follow suit. Maybe the most interesting positive effect concerns price sensitivity. Especially for brands experiencing tough competition from private labels at supermarkets, this can be very lucrative. The commercial effects of the TapForward Model trump those of the emotional model, even over time. So, why do not all brands use the TapForward Model? Well, there are a couple of reasons.

The TapForward Communication Model's business effects (Source: For the Short and Long of it)

The short-term results are a first reason why. The Rational Communication Model entails the fastest results, whereas the TapForward Model usually needs some time to reach its full effect. It works best in the middle- and long run. The results of the Rational Communication Model start to drop after six months, just when the TapForward Model shifts into action. According to Field and Binet, the effects of the two models do indeed cross each other at this six month waypoint.[152]

That is why it is so important to, just like John Lewis, combine a TapForward campaign with an activation campaign according to the 60/40 rule. You kill two birds with one stone.

A second reason is the strong correlation between creativity and the TapForward Model. Campaigns known for their creative quality are twice as able to initiate the TapForward effect. If we want to get people to talk, we will have to dare to be creative. And this is what makes it difficult. It is an art, rather than a science. Not everyone dares to take the risk to try and get the effect to take place. It takes courage. The other models are safer and easier. Two brands that did have the courage, though, are T-Mobile in the UK and Spies Travel in Denmark.

DANCING WITH T-MOBILE'S DANCE

In 2008, recession hit the UK. It was the direct consequence of the financial crisis. Many Britons swore off their phones, resulting in a 30% drop in usage. This was mainly felt in the subscription counts: people were switching over to prepaid to avoid the monthly recurring invoice. The answer of mobile providers came fast and was not unexpected at all. They lowered their prices, sometimes drastically.

T-Mobile was a small player, having a market share of merely 14%.[153] Their brand relevance was also lower than the three big players. The company was not faring well. Its three big rivals had more money, could offer lower prices and were considered more by consumers. T-Mobile could in no way keep up with a price war, as it would completely drain the company.

The first quarter of the year was when it all needed to happen. This is when subscriptions are renewed or signed. With a subscription, people get a phone, for an all-inclusive profitable price. Knowing the phone is only paid back by September, how did T-Mobile properly prepare itself for that first quarter?

A recession is a time in which people's heads are down. Everything they read on news sites or social media confirms what they are thinking already: times are tough. And the tougher the times, the more people are looking for something that makes them feel good again. This can be anything. A great film, a nice night out with friends, a good joke.

From T-Mobile's research it seemed that phones played a lead part in all this, as people shared their good times with each other over their phones. 'Life's for sharing': T-Mobile realized this was how they could make a difference. While the big three players were fighting their price wars, T-Mobile could side with emotion and try and forge a positive connection with the consumer. The company decided to go for the TapForward effect. There was no alternative: if they wanted to say that life was meant to be shared, then the campaign needed to lead by example. The story goes as follows:

Liverpool Street Station, the 15th of January 2009, at eleven in the morning. Suddenly, music sounded in the station: 'Shout' by Lulu & the Luvvers. Someone started to dance. A few notes later 'The Only Way is Up' by Yazz started playing. Some other people started dancing, then came 'Don't Cha' by the Pussycat Dolls. More people started moving, all dancing the same dance. It looked like a planned event, but the crowd seemed to like it anyway. Some people were already clapping or swaying along. Next, there was a piece of classical music. 350 people started to dance in pairs.[154] After the classical music, silence sounded. Maybe it was over? Not before 'Get Down on It' played through the station. The crowd went a bit wild. Something was cooking. People were whistling. Others joined the group and danced along. 'My Boy Lollipop' started. People got louder, they sang along. 'Do You Love Me', with all its ooh's and aahh's, was loudly chanted along too. The station was on fire. It was a flash mob. One of the best. People were taking pictures with their phones, calling their friends: 'You will never guess what just happened...' Until suddenly the music stopped. After a second, the campaign slogan appeared: 'Life is for sharing'. It was a two minute celebration of the joy of life.

That was the commercial, but there was more. In total there was six hours' worth of footage from the entire event. During the next three months, the material was made into videos, posters and communication material for retail. A YouTube channel was set up where all of the footage was shared. Bloggers and journalists were notified of the event, of which a great deal were present at the time of the flash mob. They wrote about it. It was talked about in the evening news on six different channels. Fourteen papers wrote about it as well and the event was discussed on several radio stations.[155] All before the commercial was even aired on TV 36 hours later.

After the launch of the spot, the party really started. The Sun headed: 'Feel-good telly ad everyone is watching online' and called it an 'Epidemic of joy'. 68 Facebook groups were created. The dance commercial was watched over 20 million times on YouTube. The 'Life's for sharing' channel became the second biggest UK channel on the website. Two and a half thousand bloggers wrote about it too, adding up to an estimated overall value of 1.2 million pounds worth of free media. The dance idea was copied everywhere, in schools, at weddings, even Oprah Winfrey and Beyoncé participated in the conversation. T-Mobile had obviously hit a sensitive chord. And they managed to get everyone to talk about it.

Did it pay off? Well, it brought more people to the T-Mobile stores, twice as many actually, compared to the first quarter of 2008. Sales went up by 49%.

At the same time the market only grew by 1%, T-Mobile's market share went up by 6%. T-Mobile had completely taken over the first quarter.[156] It had the courage to stand up to the top three, but whereas they chose to appeal to System 2, T-Mobile went straight for System 1. Straight for the TapForward effect. It touched the public in the right way and the campaign was shared and viewed on a massive scale. The idea was copied multiple times over and it all resulted in raising sales immediately.

DO IT FOR DENMARK

The TapForward Model can also work without the big media and production budgets, as Spies, a Danish travel agency, has proved. Spies started out in 1956 and grew to become the biggest travel agency in Denmark. The Danes grew up with their 'city breaks' and other holiday packages.

However, with the rise of the internet and low-cost airlines, more and more Danes were starting to book their holidays themselves. The market for holiday packages was stagnating. The bookings at Spies decreased by 3% between 2011 and 2013. The company needed to take action, but only had a small budget. It needed to be creative and go all out. To do so, Spies chose the TapForward Model.

The video, published online, looked at the problem in a very original way. In the style of a documentary, it called upon the Danish people to have more sex. Because as it seemed, Denmark was suffering from an insufficient birth rate. In 2013, the country even had the lowest number of childbirths in 27 years. This could not end well. Fortunately, going out of town, going on a city trip, seemed to inspire the Danes: they had 46% more sex when they were away on holiday. Spies therefore called on all Danish people to go on city trips more often. Not for Spies, but for Denmark. If a couple went on a city break with Spies and came back pregnant, they could even win three years' worth of free diapers.

It worked. 'Do It For Denmark' was viewed over 300,000 times within 24 hours. In total, the spot got ten million times views on YouTube. It was mentioned and discussed on all important news sites and in the papers. It got nearly 300,000 likes on Facebook and inspired about 500,000 comments. All of the sharing, reacting and discussing on social media and news sites together was worth as much as a media investment of 400,000 euros. The actual investment was 61,380 euros.[157] Did it rake in more sales? Yes, the sale of city breaks rose by 15.8%. Spies was so happy with the campaign they kept on working with the same model.

WHAT DO THESE CAMPAIGNS HAVE IN COMMON?

John Lewis, Spies and T-Mobile all manage to get people to discuss their campaigns on a large scale. The Fearless Girl-campaign did the same, as well as Cadbury's and Dove's, continually translating into nice commercial results.

All of these campaigns seem entirely different, but they do have certain qualities in common, both in terms of content and form. This might not be quite noticeable at first, but it becomes clear if we read between the lines. Which is exactly what we are about to do in chapter five.

CHAPTER 5

THE FRAMEWORK OF THE TAPFORWARD MODEL

'THE SCARCEST COMMODITY

IN THE 21ST CENTURY IS ATTENTION.'

THOMAS DAVENPORT

'It's the kind of thing that comedians joke about' is how Les Binet describes the TapForward campaigns.[158] Particular to the TapForward effect is that it creates an upwards participation spiral. It usually starts with paid media, but then quickly jumps over to social media, because the consumer wants to have his say about it. When there is enough buzz, the press will catch wind of it as well and journalists will start reporting on it. The more journalists write about it, the more consumers, hearing about it for the first time, will look it up. They too will want to share their opinion, because by now, it has become big news. Enter the parodies, at least if the subject allows for it. What started as a campaign has become 'the talk of the town', inciting curiosity in even the last few oblivious consumers. Hence, a positive spiral effect.

So, what is the recipe? How do you create a TapForward effect? What happens between step one, consumers seeing something for the first time, and step two, their immediate and massive response to it? All of the ingredients are to be found in the psychology of sharing: it all starts with the triggers that make people share and discuss something.

THE PSYCHOLOGY OF SHARING

Let us say the president of the United States says or does something unexpected. How we react, differs from one person to the next. Some will comment on it. Some will share that comment. Some will look for a press article, copy the URL and post without comment. Some will clearly voice whether they are for or against, while others will go looking for memes, preferring not to voice what they are thinking, instead sharing someone else's message with a twist.

The list goes on, but the point is this: what count are people and how they feel about things, not the brand and the message it wishes to convey. What people want to share with others is what really matters. This is an important observation, albeit not an easy one for marketeers.

Wanting to voice an opinion is only one of the triggers for sharing behaviour, however. Research by the New York Times brought to light some more triggers for sharing as well.[159]

Why people tap content forward?

CREATE VALUE FOR OTHERS · CREATE VALUE FOR OURSELVES · MAINTAIN RELATIONSHIPS · FIND APPRECIATION · BECAUSE IT IS IMPORTANT

The five triggers for people to tapforward content (Source: *New York Times*)

To create value for others

Although it might come as a surprise to some, a lot of people share things not to achieve fame or glory but to pass something along they think will be of value to someone else. This can be just about anything; life hacks are a prime example. The goal is clear: you just found a way to do something faster or better and you want to share this with your friends.

Funny films and memes are often shared for the same reason: you recently enjoyed yourself and wish the same for someone else. You have been served an amazing dish and want to share it through Instagram with your friends, so they can enjoy it with you. In other words: sharing is caring.

To create value for ourselves

Some of us share for their fifteen minutes of fame, like sharing pictures of food on Instagram to let friends know you can afford a three star restaurant, sharing the view from your hotel room to show you grant yourself an expensive vacation or sharing the speech of a politician to make clear which side you are on. We share to position ourselves.

To maintain relationships

We have all been there: you just posted something on Facebook and someone you have not seen in ages likes your post. This is basically the equivalent of saying a quick hello. Your friend is showing that he or she still thinks of you. So what do you do? You return the gesture, indirectly greeting each other.

Another good reason for sharing: making sure your friends do not forget about you.

To find appreciation

Getting a 'thumbs up' or, even better, a share can be such a nice feeling. Sometimes you just need a token of appreciation. You share something clever, funny or emotional to get a friendly pat on the back. 'Oh, how pretty.' 'Wow, very clever.' 'Haha, so funny'. What you're sharing is of no importance, but the recognition is. 'Wow, you still look just as young'.

Because it is important

We often share something because we deem it important: an article on global warming, homeless people and the first cold of winter, not nearly enough people donate blood… You share your support, because you consider it necessary: it is of importance for yourself, for your fellow humans, your country, the world. Getting reactions is nice, but in this case, that is not really the point. What matters most is that you have shown where you stand.

CHOOSE YOUR TRIGGER FOR SHARING

Creating value for others and creating something people deem important are the most effective triggers when it comes to getting people talking about a campaign. People will talk about or share a campaign that makes them laugh. They want to share that moment of joy with others. It is about creating value for others. The Cadbury gorilla is a good example, 'Do It for Denmark' is another. The trigger for sharing #ManOnTheMoon was different: you shared #ManOnTheMoon because it voiced an opinion that was your own and you wanted people to hear it.

The first step in designing a TapForward campaign is to decide on the trigger for sharing. This, of course, is the complete opposite of the way most campaigns have been conceived in the past and still are at present. Today our focus lies solely on how to get the message across. A very important question indeed, but it must not be the first and only one. We not only need to think about how to get the message across, but also how to get people to talk about it. Therefore, we need to integrate one of the triggers in our campaigns. If not, the only way you will activate the TapForward effect is by sheer and utter luck.

SOME EMOTIONS ARE TAPFORWARD, OTHERS ARE NOT

Have you ever talked to a friend about a sales activation? You probably have not. Even if you have, it probably was a sales activation campaign with an emotional twist to it. Do not feel bad, it is completely normal. Look again at the psychological triggers for sharing: each and every one of them are emotional.

According to the Harvard Business Review, when Dove's Real Beauty Sketches campaign went viral, it garnered nearly thirty million views in ten days. Additionally, it single-handedly added over 15,000 YouTube-subscribers to Dove's channel over the following two months, not to mention substantial increases in followers on Twitter and Facebook.[160] The emotion this campaign was built on must have been very shareable. Which begs the question: does it matter which emotion a campaign is built on? Or does it suffice to be emotional?

The eight basic emotions according to Robert Plutchik

Of course it matters, after all some emotions are far more TapForwardable than others. Robert Plutchik, professor emeritus at the Albert Einstein College of Medicine and adjunct[161] professor at the University of South Florida, is known for his wheel of emotions. He suggested eight primary bipolar emotions: joy versus sadness, anger versus fear, trust versus disgust and surprise versus anticipation. These eight primary emotions serve as the foundation of all others. They can be expressed at different intensities and can combine with one another to form different emotions.

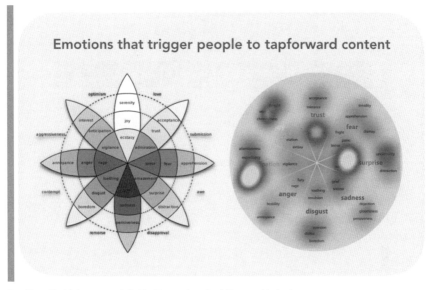

Emotions that trigger people to TapForward content (Source: *Nudge*)

In 2013, researchers examined which of the eight primary emotions were the drivers of content sharing.[162] They found that specific emotions were common in highly shared content. Particularly joy, anticipation, trust and surprise were shown to work well. Emotions that fit into the surprise and anticipation segments were overwhelmingly represented. Specifically:

- curiosity
- amazement
- interest
- astonishment
- uncertainty

Other emotions that correlated well with shareable content were:

- amusement
- happiness
- delight
- pleasure
- hope
- affection
- excitement

THE TOP 10 TAPFORWARD EMOTIONS

1. Amusement
2. Interest
3. Surprise
4. Happiness
5. Delight

6. Pleasure
7. Joy
8. Hope
9. Affection
10. Excitement

The emotions that correlate best with tapforwarded content (Source: Fractl)

The emotions that did not drive sharing were:

- anger
- politeness
- frustration
- doubt
- embarrassment
- despair
- hurt
- guilt
- contempt
- shame

Some emotions are more TapForwardable than others. So, as well as having to decide on a trigger, you have to decide on a shareable emotion, to increase your chances of activating the TapForward effect.

We immediately understand that specific triggers go hand in hand with specific emotions. If we share content because we want to create value for others, the emotions involved are to be found in the 'Joy' and 'Surprise' segments, whereas the 'Because it is important to me' trigger works well with the emotions in the 'Anticipation' and 'Trust' segments.

BRANDS ARE OPEN SOURCE

By now you surely understand that the way TapForward campaigns are designed differs from the way we used to create campaigns. We need to decide on the trigger we want to use to activate the effect. We also need to work with an emotion that fits with the trigger, otherwise the effect might not take off.

This approach is new to us. Also, some of us will just not be willing to embrace the new approach. They will be afraid consumers might turn against their brands and that the TapForward effect might create a giant PR disaster. Others like to think they still hold all the cards and, thus, they alone can decide on how their brands are positioned and perceived.

Today's consumers do not need to be taken by the hand to form their perceptions about a brand, nor will they ask our permission to start a tweet storm. Today brands are open source.

'The term "open source" refers to something people can modify and share because its design is publicly accessible', says opensource.com about the software on their website.[163] *The Cambridge Dictionary* describes it as: 'Open-source software is free to use, and the original programme can be changed by anyone.' The same goes for brands. In order for us to understand how this works, we need to take another look at how our brains work.

Kahneman tells us that brands can create mental frameworks in our brains, a kind of referencing frameworks in System 1. If this is sturdy, then the Automatic Pilot will keep choosing the same brand again and again, the Lazy Thinker will not interfere.

Who influences brand perception?

Imagine this framework as a little room inside the consumer's head. Empty at the beginning, some furniture is added when a consumer stumbles upon an ad. Now, there is a table and a chair. Every time the consumer uses the brand, the room gets dressed up a bit more, the walls get painted for example. If the same consumer praises the brand to a colleague at the coffee machine, then a comfy sofa is delivered to the room. Once it is completely decorated, it has a certain style, there is a certain feel to it.

If the consumer does not come into contact with that brand for a while, however, some things start to disappear from the room. The sofa disappears, the light switches off. So, it is important that we help the consumer keep the room well-equipped. Likewise, our rival's room should not become too pretty, it must not become the consumer's new favorite.

The marketeer helps decorate the room. Help is the critical word here, because the consumer is in control. He or she asks for advice from friends, reads comments from strangers, stumbles upon other brands in stores or online, tries things, etc. So, a brand can definitely be seen as open-source software: the code is public, and everyone can change it.

Whether marketeers want it or not, they have to accept this truth, which also rang true in the past. Though in the past marketeers had more power over the code: social media did not exist, the internet did not exist and consumers did not have the platforms they now have to share their opinions and read thousands of others.

Knowing all this, is it wise to open the door to consumer responses? Is it smart to create campaigns designed to get consumers to react? What if the reactions are negative? What if these negative reactions get amplified by the technology and platforms at hand? Is this not dangerous? Will it not put us at risk of destroying all of our cozy rooms in the heads of our consumers?

A Facebook campaign made by Dove getting the negative network effect (Source: NBC)

Well, you have no control at all, and that is exactly why you need to go looking for reactions. Let me clarify. At the time of writing this, there is a huge turmoil surrounding a Facebook advert from Dove. In this ad, a black woman turns into a white one, who then turns into a Latina. The image going around the world, however, is the one of the black woman turning into the white one, the Latina woman is left out. All hell has broken loose. Racism! No respect for diversity! I will never buy Dove again! Is this fair? Not at all, but the world simply is not. One does wonder what the company was thinking: risk-versus-reward-wise, it did not make sense. However, if you watch the full advert, you realize that the only thing Dove wanted to say was their lotion suits all skin types.

What did Dove do in this situation? Whine and complain? Claim the image going around the world had been manipulated? Not at all. They apologized and retracted everything as quickly as possible.

Nonetheless, Dove's marketeers were surely banging their heads against the wall. How did they not see this coming? Their intention has always been good and ethically praiseworthy. Was it not Dove who stood at the helm of the diversity debate? Was it not Dove who challenged photoshopping practices in an online video? Has this all been nullified by one Facebook advert? Is the room now completely collapsing?

Of course not. Luckily, the brand has been building credit in the debate for years, which is partly why many people started to defend the company. Notably, these included the black model from the advert, who spoke out in *The Guardian*: 'If I had even the slightest inclination that I would be portrayed as inferior, or as the "before" in a before and after shot, I would have been the first to say an emphatic "no". I would have (un)happily walked right off set and out of the door. That is something that goes against everything I stand for.'[164] About the negative reactions, she diplomatically said: 'The narrative has been written without giving consumers context on which to base an informed opinion.'

Is this the first time this happened to Dove? No. Will it be the last? Definitely not.

As said before: brands are open-source and that is exactly why they need to be proactive, goodwill and credit, preparing them for anything that might go wrong. Dove's current campaign strategy started in 2005, but let us first go back to the company's early days.

Dove's story starts in 1957. It was then just a successful brand of soap, first conquering America, then the world. However, around the turn of the century, selling soap amounted to merely half of all commercial results. Dove had, with time, become much more than a soap brand. But the consumer still perceived it that way. This needed to change, because it was obstructing further growth.

Sales pointed to potential in hair and skin care, but this was an entirely different category in the consumer mindset of the time. Skin care had nothing to do with cleaning yourself, but with beauty, a luxury. So, Dove wanted to become a cosmetics brand, even though the last thing the world needed was another one. There were a dime a dozen already. Still, it needed to happen for Dove to remain successful.

Dove started digging and found a way in. The beauty adverts all showed skinny, twenty-year-old models portraying an unworldly image by beauty. This is unattainable for most of the women buying their products. Advertisements by beauty brands have been having a negative effect on women, as worldwide research confirms, making them feel like a mortal in the company of the gods, or substandard goods, if you will.[165] Dove saw an opportunity in taking a stand and siding with the consumer.

The brand wanted to go the opposite direction and reinforce female confidence. It declared what would go down into history as the Dove Beauty Theory:

'Dove makes it clear it sees beauty in imperfections and does not worship stereotypes. Dove's beauty is self-defined, beauty with brains, democratic. Dove recognizes not only the exterior, but also the woman within. There is depth of character behind the eyes, strength and personality showing through.'[166]

How could this be translated into advertising? The first campaign, called 'Campaign For Real Beauty', was meant to launch the debate about beauty. With this, Dove purposely stirred the debate. The brand knew that consumers would be divided but was not afraid of negative backlash. It wanted to start a debate about what beauty means today and add their own positive contribution. It would have to be a debate in which the women's confidences were boosted. If this worked, they would have succeeded and Dove would have decorated a very pretty room in the minds of women all over the world. A much nicer room than the ones furnished by other brands in the industry. If this worked, the brand would finally be able to shake off its perception of being just a soap brand.

It worked. The campaign stirred a lot of debate, in the press, on TV, on the internet. If the company were to have added up all the free media attention, the value was estimated at around 21.4 million dollars, amounting to 150% of the original budget Dove set aside.

Adverts from the Dove Campaign for Real Beauty (Source: Ogilvy)

What about the impact on sales? In the end, this was a brand building campaign in which no products were ever shown. But of course it helps if people like Oprah Winfrey step into the debate and say things like: 'I'm gonna go get me a bar of Dove soap right now.'[167] In 2005, Dove sold 20% more than the year before and yet another 7.3% in 2006.

Brands are open-source. We do not control what the consumer will think of them or how they influence the perceptions held by other consumers. That is exactly why we need to stimulate the willingness to react, why we need to proactively look for brand activism. Dove illustrates this concept beautifully. It has been doing so for so long that it can deal with mishaps like the one we elaborated on, without unrepairable damage.

If brands are open-source, this also means every brand is subject to the Tap-Forward effect. If it's going by unnoticed, this means the effect is currently very small. To ignite it, we need to understand what the rooms in consumers' heads look like. We need to dissect them: What conversations are consumers having about the brand? What is the dominant opinion? What is the prevailing sentiment? etc. We need to understand what the room looks like and decide where it needs improvement. Subsequently, we need to work our way back in order to understand what trigger and emotion need to be created for the consumer to TapForward. If we use the open source metaphor, how do you get people to write a piece of code with necessary functionality without directly telling them they have to write it? By inspiring them.

ENGAGE TO GET ENGAGEMENT

A CEO's job is to execute his plan, the one he presented to the stockholders, within the agreed upon time and budget. He cannot do this alone, he needs people. His success is undeniably connected to how well he can inspire and motivate his people to execute the plan. There are two ways to do this.

One way is the conventional way. In a PowerPoint presentation explaining the plan step by step in elaborate detail, the importance of every step highlighted with figures and statistics. It is an intellectual appeal that leaves you neither hot nor cold. It is a task that needs to be completed. The presentation only serves to pass on the information people need to successfully fulfill the task.

What happens in the minds of the public during such a presentation? One half cannot read the numbers because there are too many on one slide and loses track of the story. What they hear is a to-do list. The other half can read the numbers but has its reservations. They already see what will not work, exceeding the things that will work out by far. Their attention starts waning. At the end of the presentation, everyone returns to their desks, the weight on their shoulders heavier than before.

So, best choose the inspiring way. Executives who manage to set the whole room aflame quickly outgrow their presentation. They do not talk about numbers, they have a story to tell. They are on a mission and invite you in. Their enthusiasm is contagious and after fifteen minutes, smiles grace the faces of half the crowd.

The CEO's story is full of emotion. There is no beating about the bush: it will not be easy to execute the project. It is going to be a bumpy ride, with twists and turns that might make you sick to your stomach, but it will work out. The CEO emphasizes how brilliant things will be when it all works out. Employees hang onto every word, applauding from sheer enthusiasm when it all ends, going back to their desks invigorated. The weight on their shoulders has become less because they feel inspired and engaged. They are aware that it might get tough, but they know they can rely on their CEO who is super engaged.

What applies to a CEO, applies to a marketeer as well. If we want the consumer to follow us, we have to inspire them to take action. We do not 'inform' people to take action, we inspire them. What is the mission we are putting forward? How can consumers get involved? How can we connect them to our message emotionally? And finally: what is the engagement that we will take upon ourselves? What is our brand's engagement?

Faking engagement is impossible

Whereas Coca-Cola strives for the perception of timelessness, Pepsi has always tried to be the 'in the moment' brand. The cool, contemporary brand, that understands the needs of today. In April 2017, Pepsi launched a new TV commercial: 'Jumpin In', a clear attempt to ride the wave for harmony among people. 'Pepsi is trying to project a global message of unity, peace and understanding', the brand said.[168]

The advert showed a protest march. People of different skin colours, gender and talents were walking behind boards, depicting slogans like 'Peace' and

'Join the conversation'. The crowd passed by a model posing for a photoshoot, which turned out to be Kendall Jenner. She curiously looked at the crowd. There was a cellist, who stopped playing to look outside. A photographer noticed the crowd of passers-by as well. Both decided to walk along, while Kendall kept posing. At some point, however, she grew tired of it as well, taking off her wig, rubbing off her lipstick and joining the crowd. She took a can of Pepsi and walked towards police officers wanting to stop the protest. She handed one of them the can. The crowd erupted in cheers as he took a sip. 'Live bolder, live louder', appeared on the screen. The ad was signed 'Live for now'.

Did this commercial bring people together? Indeed, it did. All over the internet people came together in loud protest against Pepsi's failed attempt at giving itself purpose, at trying to call for social change. The criticism was harsh. 'Stupefyingly diabolical', 'dumb' and 'disrespectful' were used to describe the ad on Twitter.[169] People said Pepsi was blind to what was really going on and trying to recruit the Black Lives Matter movement. Even Martin Luther King's son tweeted with a great deal of cynicism: 'If only daddy would have known about the power of #Pepsi.'[170] Less than 24 hours later, Pepsi had to recall the commercial and apologize. Pepsi failed to connect to what society finds important. It failed to inspire and engage people for its cause because there was no cause. Its engagement was totally fake and people found it offensive.

Let us compare with another – quite unexpected – brand that tried to rally people to its cause: Persil.

Thirteen years ago, Persil launched the Dirt is Good Campaign in the UK. It was a complete turnaround for the brand, going from: 'We will make sure that you can wash your kids' clothes whiter than white' to: 'It is good that your kids get dirty, it means they had fun and learned something new'. What Persil did to dirty clothes is a bit similar to what Dove did with their campaign about real beauty. The brand changed the meaning of 'dirty clothes', making it more synonymous with a kid's positive development, and less so with the time wasted by yet another load of dirty laundry. And it worked: sales soared.

However, by 2015 the effect was wearing off. The decrease in Persil's brand relevance was worrisome. The Dirt is Good story seemed to have reached its expiry date. Or had it? Parents still stood behind the message, but the story was just not relevant anymore: the time children spend playing outside has been cut by half over the past fifteen years. Not because parents do not want their kids playing outside anymore, but why would you go outside if you have access to Google, YouTube, Facebook or Twitch (basically an endless virtual playground) right in the palm of your hand? However, according to many studies, this societal trend has negatively impacted today's teenagers's health, so Persil decided to up the stakes. It wanted to take on an activist role and try to turn the trend around. A very ambitious goal for a detergent brand, and not one without risk.

The campaign was launched in 2016. It started with a mini documentary, available online and in cinemas. It showed images of a prison: the Wabash Maximum Security Prison in the American state of Indiana. Prisoners talked about how it feels to lose your freedom, to be locked up. It is maddening to be in constant confrontation with your own thoughts, they claimed.

The inmates talked about the thing they look forward to most: the two hours a day they were allowed to go outside, stressing the importance of being able to escape the four walls of their cell. They were asked how they would feel if the two hours outside would be cut by half. 'Torture', one of the prisoners said. 'Disastrous', a prison guard stated.

Next, they were asked if they knew who goes outside only one hour a day. Some faces of disbelief appeared. People cannot possibly be allowed only one hour outside a day? The answer remained unclear, until the interviewer answered it himself: kids. 'That's depressing', one of the inmates replied. 'I do not even know what to say to that', another one said. On the screen a figure appeared: 'On average, children now spend less time outdoors than a prison inmate.' 'Something has gone very wrong', viewers heard an inmate say. The commercial was signed 'Free the kids' and #DirtIsGood.

Additionally, the campaign consisted of a collaboration with Sir Ken Robinson, a world-renowned expert on the development of children. On YouTube and Periscope, he talked about why it is important for kids to play outside and he offered some guidelines. In cooperation with schools, Empty Classroom Day was launched. On this day, the 17th of June 2016, a lot of schools organized their classes outside. Also, Persil built six hundred playgrounds for kids.[171] In Vietnam, the brand even convinced the government to make it mandatory for schools to offer their students a playground.

The documentary amassed 1.4 million views on YouTube, got 22.6 million impressions on Twitter and gave 258,000 kids the opportunity to have class outside. How did consumers respond? They voted with their wallets: sales rose by 2.1%, while market share showed an increase of thirteen base points.[172] The consumer seemed to agree with Persil.

THREE LEVELS OF BRAND ENGAGEMENT

So, why did Pepsi fail where Persil won? Both are brands you would not expect to be socially engaged. There are a couple of reasons why one brand succeeded, while the other failed. It has to do with the level of engagement. There are three levels of engagement a brand can show.

The functional level

The functional level is the easiest. This is what brands do through their promotional activities: 'If you do this, then we will do that'. Buy a product, get the second one free and all related variations. The engagement that brands are looking for, in this case, is rather small and short-lived. The engagement they are showing is entirely functional, it is sales activation. The goal is to push short-term sales up on a short-term basis. However, as that does not sound all that exciting, how do you get people to talk about it?

Let us take a look at how Media Markt approached this on their German home turf. Their first store opened in 1979, promising the best prices and the sharpest discounts in the market. Their success was huge: in 2014 Media Markt was the most important brand in Germany. However, despite their online business doing well, the overhead of an expensive brick and mortar network started taking its toll and the company encountered increasing difficulty offering the lowest prices. The retailer also had to deal with showrooming: people came to the stores to check out products in real life, only to then buy them online. Media Markt needed to turn the tide. Easter holiday 2015 seemed like a perfect time to launch an attack, but how?

Research shows that a great deal of consumers spend a lot of time comparing prices and analyzing offers, which takes them way more time than the couple of euros they gain from it. Media Markt nonetheless tried to understand the phenomenon and quickly realized that comparing prices and offers has all sorts of game-like features. The essence of the game is: how can I beat the system? Or how can I outsmart commercial companies? The game turns out to be more important than the result. The thrill is in the game, not in saving a few bucks.

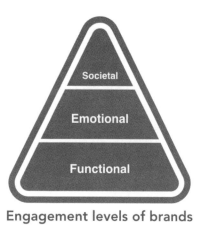

Engagement levels of brands

Societal

Emotional

Functional

Levels of brand engagement

A valuable insight, so it seemed, but could Media Markt use it to activate its audience and boost sales? The brand launched 'The Rabbit Race', a running competition for Easter bunnies, broadcast live with comments by Germany's most famous sports journalist Frank Buschmann. The campaign unfolded in different phases.

During the first phase, the 'athletes' were introduced through press conferences and every bunny got its own Facebook page. There even a follow-up on Twitter, all as if were truly a real-world championship or some other big sports event. The goal clearly was to make people talk about the event: Media Markt wanted to raise its brand notoriety and consideration to a higher level, just in time for the sales period.[173]

A couple of days before the first race, the second phase kicked off. Every purchase receipt at Media Markt was numbered: consumers whose receipt numbers corresponded to the winning bunny received 50% off their original purchase. Three races were broadcasted live on nine TV stations at the same time, as well as on YouTube. Some 21 million Germans were live-watching the spectacle. In comparison, the semi-final between the Netherlands and Argentina for the 2014 FIFA World Cup amassed only 19.5 million German viewers. On social media there was a lot of buzz as well: compared to the Easter period of 2014, the amount of Facebook followers rose by 350%, the number of social interactions increased by 114% and the total Twitter followers by 200%. After the start of the races, the number of searches mentioning Media Markt on Google went up by 50%.

Did it also get Media Markt more customers? As a matter of fact, there was an increase of 18.2% compared to a year earlier, with the average receipt up 13%. The revenue in the Easter period grew by 25%.[174] Hence, Media Markt showed that even a sales activation can engage people. Even though the promotion was very tactical and reasoned in itself, it was delivered in a way that fed System 1: the campaign was shared and talked about, because it built on the 'Create value for others' trigger and the emotion focused on was Joy. This explains why a larger number of people visited the stores and left with more purchases.

The emotional level

Appealing on an emotional level is a little trickier. What it boils down to is an honest laugh or tear that will have your consumer go straight to Facebook and proclaim how good it was. These are no regular stories, this is not just crude humour but stories that move people so much they will continue to talk about them.

An example. We already elaborated on John Lewis' Man On The Moon campaign, now let us take a look at another one of their ads: #MontyThePenguin, the 2014 Christmas campaign.

On the 6th of November 2014, the campaign started with the launch of a TV commercial. In less than an hour after the online launch, the spot appeared at the top of Twitter's trending list. Within 48 hours, it had been tweeted about 124,000 times. The ad was the talk of the town, not just on Twitter. John Lewis' 'Word of Mouth' value (the extent a brand is talked about offline or online) increased by 71%.

What story was John Lewis telling and what made the public take action that fast? It was the story of an unusual friendship between Sam, a young boy, and Monty, a penguin. Sam and Monty were inseparable. They played hide and seek together, jumped on trampolines together, played football together, ate together and so on. Everything they did, they did together. Yet, when first snowfall and the unpacking of the Christmas tree set in, Sam noticed his companion seemed a bit blue, especially when he saw two people lovingly kiss each other. Sam understood Monty was feeling lonely, missing the company of another penguin. When they woke up on Christmas day, Sam had a surprise in store. Both of them went down to the living room, Sam covering Monty's eyes. What did Monty see when Sam took away his hands? Another penguin. Monty was ecstatic!

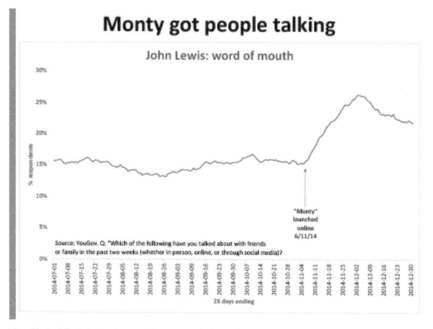

The effect of the John Lewis campaign on Word of Mouth (Source: Les Binet, adam&eve DBB)

All the while, Mum was standing in the doorway and saw Sam playing with two penguin dolls, making them kiss each other. Sam seemed delighted with his Christmas present. 'Give someone the Christmas they have been dreaming of', appeared above the image of happy Sam.

The existential theme John Lewis chose clearly was friendship. Real, honest, loyal friendship. The emotion viewers identified with was sadness. Monty was sad because he did not have a penguin buddy to celebrate Christmas with, with Sam as the hero in his story. Until there was a twist in the plot line, as the new framework was shown: actually, it was all about Sam and how the boy made an imaginary friend out of his favourite plush toy Monty, both living exciting adventures. The real story was how Sam actually deemed it necessary for Monty to find a buddy for Christmas. Suddenly viewers understood that Sam was not the hero after all, his mum was. She is the one who gave Sam the gift of his dreams. It was this surprising and deeply emotional conclusion that got people to shed a tear and react.

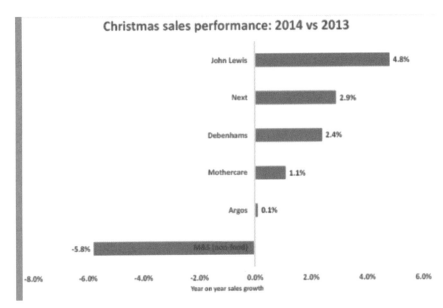

John Lewis' Christmas sales performance in 2014 (Source: Les Binet, adam&eve DDB)

All fine and dandy, you might say, but is this not the kind of story that touches people one day, only to be forgotten, brand and all, the next? Not at all. The TV commercial was but a part of a larger campaign centered around #MontyThePenguin, consisting of a carefully crafted PR campaign, a big merchandising campaign, content partnerships with Google, Channel 4 and Microsoft, posters, in-store events, even a children's book, an app and social media support. For people living in the UK, there was definitely no way to look past Monty.

How about the commercial result? 'We won Christmas', John Lewis wrote: '123 million pounds in extra sales with a net profit of 33 million pounds.' The campaign yielded eight times its production cost. Compared to its competitors, John Lewis was the most mentioned and best-selling department store in the UK during the Christmas period of 2014.[175]

As you see, if marketeers want to unlock these levels of emotional engagement, they need to put in quite some effort. Just making a commercial and being done with it, will not suffice: you need to think things through. It requires writing and constructing commercials in a way that evokes response, combined with a detailed activation campaign.

YouGov: most talked about high street retailers

Rank	Brand	Score
1	John Lewis	18.3
2	Marks & Spencer	7.5
3	Boots	6.7
4	Poundland	5.7
5	Lakeland	4.9

The most talked about retailers in 2014 (Source: Les Binet, adam&eve DBB)

The socially relevant level

Books, consultants, conferences, they all agree: brands need to have purpose. They need to define their role in society, find out how they can make the world a better place. Even though this is currently very trendy, the complexity of the matter is usually underestimated. This is the most difficult level of engagement, bearing the highest risks. However, if it does work, it is a brand's most amazing gift. It will grow stronger and sales will soar. If it does not work, however, you will be eviscerated by the press and even more so by the consumer, as happened to Pepsi. The soft drink brand will need some time to recuperate from the backlash.

As a brand addressing topics they are dead serious about, getting this right is of the utmost importance to consumers. You need to show you are equally serious. Point in case: Dove is fully committed and proves so. When watching Pepsi's commercial, however, it is obvious that they are not. They merely ticked off all the boxes. Diversity? Check. Different skin colours? Check. Gender equality? Check. Did we forget another societal trend? No? Ok, cut! From miles away it was clear that this commercial would not evoke sympathy, on the contrary, it provoked anger. The ad showed a fundamental lack of respect for all issues Pepsi tried to include. It might have gotten away with something like that in the past, but today? No way Jose.

The question of whether or not carrying out a certain social engagement fits your brand is easy to answer. What do you find most important: a better world, or a better end of year result? The diplomatic answer 'both' is not an option. If there is even the slightest hint of hesitation about the true motivation, a brand risks ending up in the eye of a (social) media storm. If you cannot wholeheartedly answer 'a better world', you need to keep away from socially relevant themes.

Some companies, such as Patagonia and Ben & Jerry's, go all out for social relevancy. Their logic is simple: they are successful and have society to thank for that. So, they consider it their duty to give back. P&G and Unilever are working on this as well, successfully: 'Fifty percent of Unilever's growth today is coming from brands that are acting on their purpose. Growth for these brands is 30% higher than the brands that did not crack the purpose', Aline Santos, Unilever's EVP Global Marketing stated at the Cannes Lions Festival in 2016. Exactly like Persil and Ben & Jerry's, it is clear that they mean business and they prove it with a variety of actions.

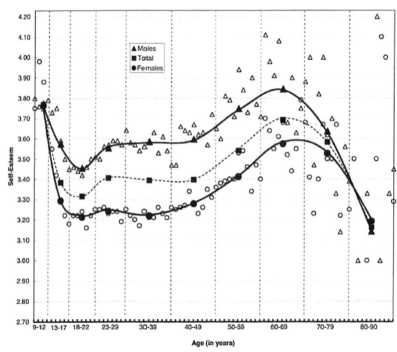

Source: 'Global Self-Esteem Across the Life Span' Study, American Psychological Association, Inc., 2002 , Vol 17, No. 3, 423 – 434

Self-esteem across one's life span (Source: warc.com)

Let us take a look at another important advertiser's brand: Always by P&G. Menstrual pads are a very functional, low-involvement product. As such, so is its advertising. Once a woman has chosen a brand, she sticks to it. Many women choose Always, as it has been worldwide category leader for years. However, among girls and women between 16 and 24 years old it has been losing relevance. A problem for the brand, exactly because of brand loyalty in the category: the brand rose to size thanks to high loyalty, but that inherently entails a huge risk of catastrophic downfall. To become relevant again with this young target group, the answer was no longer functional advertising. Instead, the Always brand needed to forge an emotional connection.

The core of the Always brand has always been trust, but on a functional level. The product does what it is supposed to do. So, the consumer can trust it to do its job. There is an emotional side to trust that goes way deeper with young women. Everyone kind of loses confidence during puberty, but young female teenagers tend to experience this a bit stronger than young men. The cause? The answer is quite obvious: gender stereotyping. The message young girls get during puberty is that strength, power and leadership are attributes typically associated with men, whereas pretty and amenable are typically female characteristics.

Research points out that parents believe boys should not be raised like girls, basically implying that being brought up as a girl is not good enough. This has negative implications for the self-worth of these young girls, especially those between ten and twelve years old.[176] In the US, this stereotyping runs deep, it is even embedded in the language. Doing something 'like a girl' implies you are bad at it.

Always saw this as an opportunity to take a socially relevant stance. To make the world a bit better by supporting teenage girls and giving them some self-confidence. The brand decided to set up an experiment. Participants thought it was a casting, with young men and women on one hand and a couple of teenage girls on the other. The assigned task was to 'run like a girl' and 'fight like a girl'. The teenagers ran and fought as hard as they could, showing pride. They gave it their everything, brimming with confidence. The somewhat older girls and boys on the other hand, did not run and fight hard at all. They ran and hit 'like a girl': childish, like a little girl, showing a good example of societal stereotyping. These youngsters were already tainted.

Always got everything out of the experiment it needed to make its point, so it subsequently did. The brand made a pre-roll video for YouTube, supplemented with Facebook and Twitter adverts, banners and collaborations with influencers. #LikeAGirl was launched. The sixty-second version was shown during the Super Bowl of 2015. The video was seen over 90 million times and shared over a million times in 28 days. The commercial hit number two in the list of worldwide viral videos. The hashtag appeared in schools and in coffee shops alike.

In the first three months, 177,000 #LikeAGirl tweets were sent. In that same period, it was mentioned over 100,000 times in the media. The total of all the media impressions amounted to over 4 billion. In March 2015, the campaign even received a United Nations award, because of its impact on female empowerment worldwide. In October 2015, US president Barack Obama honored the national women's football team in the White House, as in July that year the team beat Japan to become world champions. Obama congratulated the women and thanked them for showing American children that 'playing like a girl means you are badass'.[177]

'The Always "Like a Girl" campaign did, indeed, change the meaning of "like a girl". From only 19% of girls having a positive connotation with the phrase before the campaign to 76% post-campaign, we believe we are making a difference', Amanda Hill, P&G's brand director for Always, said during a 2016 press conference.[178] P&G never reveals sales results, so we do not know if the success translated into higher sales as well, but today, the campaign is running still. This can only mean it has yielded positive results. In September 2017 a new commercial was released: 'Keep Going'.

WHAT LEVEL OF ENGAGEMENT FITS YOUR BRAND?

The socially relevant level is not suitable for every brand. Pepsi is a great example of this, as well as a couple of other brands that tried, but failed. McDonalds in the UK is one of them.[179] Heineken with their 'Worlds Apart' campaign is another.[180] As a brand, you cannot always deal with every level of engagement, there are a couple of elements you need to keep in mind.

The DNA of your brand

Patagonia can handle the three levels of engagement because its DNA allows for it. Patagonia is an American outdoor gear and clothing brand. It strives to make its ecological footprint as small as possible. That is exactly why it calls for their consumers to buy as little as possible. Yes, you read that right. They, as a company, play their part by making their clothing last as long as possible. Their clothing is recyclable as well, so if one of their jackets is worn, the customer can return it and Patagonia will reuse the materials.[181] Clearly, Patagonia means it. For example, they called upon their consumers to not buy

Patagonia on Black Friday: in November 2011, a 'Do not buy this jacket' advert appeared in the *New York Times* on Black Friday 2011. Nobody doubts whether the company is serious or not. Their engagement is entirely on-key with how Patagonia runs its business.

Examples of brand activism (Source: Patagonia)

Someone who does not know the brand, might still have their doubts about Patagonia's engagement. But surely, knowing that the brand even stands up to its own national president dissipates all doubt? As a matter of fact, Patagonia is taking legal action against the plan of current U.S. president Donald Trump to limit the number of national parks in Utah and Nevada to 85%. The company will not hide from it: at the time of writing, their website homepage reads: 'The president stole your land'. The environment is an important cause for Patagonia. The enterprise donates 1% of its revenue every year to environmental organizations. In 2016, it even gave all of its Black Friday revenue, 10 million dollars, to these same organizations.[182]

Ben & Jerry's, a more commonly known brand in Europe compared to Patagonia, equally has a DNA allowing it to take on credible, serious engagement. Ben & Jerry's DNA is one of social activism. In July 2016, the brand launched a campaign titled 'Democracy is in your hands', a clear message calling for people to vote. They phrased it as follows:

'We believe democracy only works when it works for everyone. But lately, it seems the challenges facing our democracy have gotten out of hand: low income and minority voters are having their voting rights infringed upon, and money from wealthy donors is corrupting the system. But there is hope. Because every individual has a hand in creating democracy. Our democracy does not belong to politicians. Or businesses. Or to wealthy donors. It belongs to you.'[183]

Pretty gutsy for an ice cream brand, getting involved in the United States elections, you might think. The brand got away with it because it is part of its DNA. Democracy is not the first cause it committed to either: the fight against global warming is another one.

However, if the DNA of a brand does not allow for this kind of engagement, it had better not try and definitely should not fake it. These brands need to limit themselves to the first two levels of engagement: the functional and the emotional levels. That is okay.

THE SURPRISE PERSPECTIVE

Jean-Claude Van Damme keeps his eyes closed, arms crossed. He opens his eyes and says: 'I had my ups and downs, my fair share of bumpy roads and heavy winds. That's what made me what I am today.' The camera pans out. Van Damme seems to be standing between two driving trucks, each leg on one of the mirrors. The trucks are driving backwards. As the camera pans out further, we see the space in between the trucks increase, they are driving away from each other. The legs of the actor follow. Wider and wider. He still has his arms crossed. Even wider. You can feel the pain in your own legs. Then, he falls into the perfect T. You cannot believe your eyes, what a split, even with the trucks still driving. All the while Van Damme is hanging there, a text appears on the screen: 'This test was set up to demonstrate the stability and precision of Volvo Dynamic Steering. It was carried out by professionals.' It was a live recording.

This is an example of a surprise perspective. Or better, of a surprising change of perspective. You do not see it coming, and once you figure it out, you are so surprised you want to share it, because of all the reasons we mentioned before.

Did it work for Volvo? The 'Epic Split' film, that only appeared on YouTube, was watched 87 million times. No other YouTube video made by the car industry has done better. The video was shared 6 million times on social networks and parodied thousands of times. Together, all of the parodies reached another 50 million views. The value of all of the media attention boiled down to 87 million euros. What did it do to sales? In the fourth quarter of 2013 (right after

the campaign launch) Volvo Trucks sales went up 24%. The president and
CEO of Volvo Group, Olof Persson, at the end of 2013 said: 'Volvo Trucks has
exceeded our expectations and contributed to the Volvo brand increasing its
market share in Europe to historically high levels.'[184] A TapForward effect of
unprecedented proportions.

The surprise perspective is what makes the film so successful. Take away the
surprise and what is left is just a brand talking about a new steering system
that increases the stability of the truck. Not very exciting. Or at least not
almost 90 million views worth of excitement.

The majority of campaigns with a high TapForward effect uses this technique.
Likewise, the Always brand invited children and youngsters to act 'like a girl'
in front of the camera, only to subsequently discuss the perceived differences
between boys and girls, and their effect on girls. Dove, in turn, revealed how
the techniques of the fashion industry create false beauty ideals. John Lewis
took the perspective of a young child building an imaginary relationship with
a lonely old man on the moon. Persil fought for more freedom for kids by
letting prisoners speak. Spies used statistics on sexual activity to promote city
trips to consumers and Media Markt let bunnies race. In every one of these
cases the story was told from an uncommon perspective, stirring positive
emotions in consumers. Consumers felt their fresh and extraordinary take
was clever and they liked to share their amazement.

Whereas John Lewis' 'Man On The Moon' campaign can still be seen as a
classic advertising story building up to a climax, TapForward campaigns
increasingly steer away from the traditional format, replacing it with journal-
ism techniques such as reports, interviews, social experiments, statistics and
interpretations by experts. This 'journalistic approach' gives the campaign a
higher 'news value', which might motivate people to support the story.

Obviously, the surprise effect has been around for longer: the giants of
advertising, filmmakers and marketeers all knew it as one of the basic laws
of storytelling, along with other elements of the TapForward framework. As
such, it goes without saying we still need to think about the target group, the
consumer insight we want to work with to define the messaging platform, a
tone of voice and a media distribution plan. None of that changes. Without
them we would not be able to create campaigns, although if we were to only
use these, chances of activating the TapForward effect are slim.

Only when the choice of engagement is consciously decided upon, when the emotion it represents is at its best and when the trigger for sharing fits, do campaigns have a shot at reaching positive network effect. That positive network effect, called the TapForward effect, is inherently linked to the new operating system the world is running on today. The scale of the network effect is unprecedented, hence, so is the growth it can lead to. Therefore, aiming for this effect should be part of marketing and creative strategies.

Do not forget every brand is open source: every day some new pieces of code are being written. The TapForward effect is already happening for every brand. For those who are unaware of it, the effect is small. However, as we have seen, this can change any day and brands might not see it coming. Thus, the better strategy is to proactively ignite it.

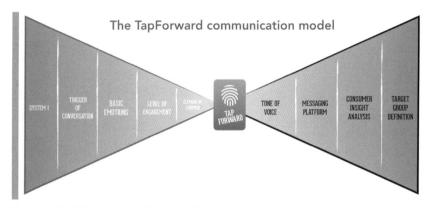

The elements of the TapForward Communication Model

CHAPTER 6

NOW WHAT?

What do we do now? Good question.

The world is running on a new operating system. We are going through a transformational phase, the end of which is not yet in sight. This digital trans- formation is giving consumers way more possibilities to escape advertising, which they are doing, on a massive scale, because of our mediocre work. Our true trade, our quality work, however, does still get us huge results every once in a while. The situation has become black and white: either your campaign barely gets noticed, or it catches on. In both cases, it is up to the consumer to decide.

Of course, even before the digital transformation some campaigns already had wide reaches thanks to consumers, but not on the scale we know today, a scale that is inherently linked to the new operating system. Just think of Fearless Girl and how consumers sent pictures of that little statue all over the world. Or the John Lewis campaigns and how they were propelled by consum- ers to higher spheres.

Another consequence of the digital transformation is the growing amount of data available to us. If we use the acquired insights to support our creativity, we can obtain absolutely mind-boggling results. After all, we have seen what The Economist managed to do.

However, the results of the digital transformation are not all positive: take the confusion we keep inflicting on ourselves. Whenever something new comes around, we proclaim the death of the old. That is why we are completely misinterpreting the power of the different media. And even though the giants of advertising invented all the important techniques, we still feel the need to keep reinventing them, wasting our energy and distracting our focus.

We have also ended up in the vicious cycle of short-term thinking, with all of its consequences. The efficiency of our campaigns is free-falling, crash- ing even, before our eyes. The more it decreases, the more we think in the short-term. The more short-term we think, the more the result decreases. And that is how we stay stuck in a negative spiral. The experts' voices are sounding clearer by the day: the scale has tipped too far to the wrong side. We know that we have to work in the short-term, as well as the long-term. We even know the right proportion: 40% of the budget needs to go towards sales activation, 60% to brand building.

We can of course ignore the experts' opinions and keep going down the same road, but we are slowly yet steadily evolving towards a world where algorithms are increasingly helping consumers choose. Algorithms are devoid of emotions: they choose the lowest price and the most favorable reviews, regardless of the brands, so we have to count on the consumer to actively choose our brands.

At the same time, a new generation is in the works: Gen Z. In two years, they will represent 40% of all consumers. They are the most tech-savvy generation yet, as well as the most demanding. They want to know what your brand stands for, what values you find important and how you will help them make the world a better place, in every way. Together with the algorithms, they form the perfect storm.

We know what to do. We need to make our brands stronger, so they can hold themselves upright when the proverbial hurricane hits. We can do this by focusing on System 1, making sure that our brands form part of the 90% of decisions we make while on Auto Pilot.

Increasingly, we also understand that it is not just about the difference between traditional or digital media, but that the essence is marketing in a digital world. So, let us sit down and talk about advertising and how we can adjust. Adjust is the key word there: we do not have to start from scratch and invent something new. Although we find loads of opinions on Google claiming that that is exactly what we should do, these are the same voices stating that TV and everything related to the past are over and done with. Maybe they need to do their homework a bit better.

Nonetheless, the truth is quite simple. If we apply Sinek's Golden Circle to our trade, we can see that surely not everything needs to change. Our 'why' has not changed. We are still looking for sustainable growth, and this will not change as long as we stay in the current economic framework. The 'what' is clear as well: content that creates short-term effects and content that creates long-term effects. That will not change any time soon either. The 'how' is evolving, however. The media platforms are in flux, though not even that is a matter of life or death: traditional and digital media complement each other quite beautifully. In fact, they reinforce each other.

The best functioning communication model in the digital world is the TapForward Model. It builds nicely on the laws of physics that were given to us by the giants of advertising and it yields strong results. Results that are way stronger than from any of the other models. We now know what the elements of the TapForward Model are and we know how to apply them.

So, what now? Try and make the TapForward Model work for your brand. Make this your prime focus, and shut out all the possible confusions throwing themselves at you.

It is time.

It is your time.

I wish you the best of luck.

OVERVIEW CASE STUDIES:

Dove, 'Evolution'
Fearless Girl, SSGA
Apple, 'Think Different'
Cadbury, Gorilla
Volkswagen, 'The Snow Plow'
The Economist, 'Raising Eyebrows'
Michelin, Le Guide Michelin
Dr. Oetker
John Deere, *The Furrow*
Burma-Shave, Verses
Philip Morris, *I Love Lucy*
Volkswagen, 'The Funeral'
AVIS, 'We Try Harder'
Axe, 'Find Your Magic'
Johnnie Walker, 'Keep Walking'
John Lewis, 'Man On The Moon'
AgeUK, 'Man On The Moon'
T-Mobile, Dance
Spies, 'Do it for Denmark'
Dove, 'Real Beauty'
Pepsi, 'Jump In'
Media Markt, 'Rabbit Race'
John Lewis, 'Monty The Penguin'
Always, 'Like A Girl'
Patagonia, 'Don't Buy this Jacket'
Ben & Jerry's, 'Democracy Is in Your Hands'

ACKNOWLEDGEMENTS

This is a book about the craft of advertising. To be able to write a book about a craft, you first need to have been taught it. I have been fortunate enough to have been trained and to have worked with a couple of giants from our industry, both in Belgium, my home country, as well as internationally. I learned the tricks of the trade from the last of the original Mad Men in Belgium: Guillaume Van der Stighelen, Patrick Willemarck and Georges Lafleur.

At the beginning of the digital revolution I had the chance to lead OgilvyInteractive in Brussels. Jan Van Aken, the CEO of Ogilvy at the time, assigned me the task of helping to build OgilvyInteractive around digital brand innovation. A couple of years later, I was able to do the same for OgilvyInteractive in Eastern Europe and Russia. There, I met Robin Weeks, the Chief Creative Officer of Ogilvy. For nights on end, together with Joseph Havelka, we scratched our heads thinking about how we could create an impact for brands in the new digital world. Not because we thought Moscow's nightlife had nothing to offer us, but because global brands were looking to us to figure this out for them. You could say that figuring out and renewing the rules of our craft has always been a passion of mine.

To Heidi Lagast, thank you for the coaching and advice during the writing process.

To Hermine Van Coppenolle, thank you for the reality check on the Gen Z research and the English translation.

And lastly, my thanks to the LannooCampus team for the trust and swift collaboration.

ABOUT THE AUTHOR

Wim Vermeulen is the director of strategy & innovation at Dentsu Aegis Network and the managing director at Dentsu Consulting. His experience over the years at the various creative bureaus, start-ups and digital agencies that he led both at home and overseas has made him a tried and tested entrepreneur, as well as an expert on digital transformation and brand innovation.

As a political scientist with a masters degree in communication sciences, he is a popular keynote speaker and lectures at Solvay Business School. He studied management and marketing strategy at the universities of Oxford and Cambridge.

END NOTES

1. Robinson, M. How To Create Modern Advertising That Sells. 27 Sept. 2015, www.medium.com/swlh/how-to-create-modern-advertising-that-sells-c9f37c8a4b38 (Accessed 4 Jul. 2017).

2. Beer, J. What Happened To All The Funny Ads? 8 Sept. 2017, www.fastcompany.com/40449835/what-happened-to-all-the-funny-ads (Accessed 8 Sept. 2017).

3. Lim, J. Don't Forget to Sell - The Unchanging and Changing Nature of Advertising. 9 Jun. 2016, www.fastcompany.com/40449835/what-happened-to-all-the-funny-ads (Accessed 2 Feb. 2017).

4. Pingdom, How we got from 1 to 162 million websites on the internet. 4 Apr. 2008, www.royal.pingdom.com/2008/04/04/how-we-got-from-1-to-162-million-websites-on-the-internet/ (Accessed 5 Jul. 2017).

5. Internet Live Stats, Total number of Websites. www.internetlivestats.com/total-number-of-websites/ (Accessed 5 Jul. 2017).

6. Soper, T. Amazon Echo sales reach 5M in two years, research firm says, as Google competitor enters market. 21 Nov. 2016, www.geekwire.com/2016/amazon-echo-sales-reach-5m-two-years-research-firm-says-google-competitor-enters-market/ (Accessed 5 Jul. 2017).

7. Johnson, L. Coca-Cola Wants to Use AI Bots to Create Its Ads. 28 Feb. 2017, www.adweek.com/digital/coca-cola-wants-to-use-ai-bots-to-create-its-ads/ (Accessed 5 Jul. 2017).

8. Marshall, A. From Jingles to Pop Hits, A.I. Is Music to Some Ears. 22 Jan. 2017, www.nytimes.com/2017/01/22/arts/music/jukedeck-artificial-intelligence-songwriting.html?_r=0 (Accessed 6 Jul. 2017).

9. Kurzweil, R. The Law of Accelerating Returns. 7 Mar. 2001, www.kurzweilai.net/the-law-of-accelerating-returns (Accessed 1 Jul. 2017).

10. Urban, T. The AI Revolution: The Road to Superintelligence. 22 Jan. 2015, www.waitbutwhy.com/2015/01/artificial-intelligence-revolution-1.html (Accessed 2 Jul. 2017).

11. Moore, G. Cramming More Components onto Integrated Circuits. 1 Jan. 1998, www.cs.utexas.edu/~fussell/courses/cs352h/papers/moore.pdf (Accessed 2 Jul. 2017).

12. Ford, M. (2015). *The rise of the robots*. London: Oneworld Publications.

13. Sandoval, G. Former Blockbuster CEO tells his side of Netflix story. 22 Jan. 2015, www.cnet.com/news/former-blockbuster-ceo-tells-his-side-of-netflix-story/ (Accessed 2 Jul. 2017).

14. Miller, G. Here's How People 100 Years Ago Thought We'd Be Living Today. 28 May 2014, www.wired.com/2014/05/victorian-postcards-pre-dict-future/#slide-2 (Accessed 3 Jul. 2017).

15. Wikipedia. Charging Bull. 29 Jul. 2017, www.nl.wikipedia.org/wiki/Charging_Bull (Accessed 1 Aug. 2017).

16. Whiteside, S. How the "Fearless Girl" helped State Street Global Advisors find its voice. Jun. 2017, www.warc.com/SubscriberContent/Article/How_the_'Fearless_Girl'_helped_State_Street_Global_Advisors_find_its_voice/111702 (Accessed 10 Jul. 2017).

17. Komolafe, T. 'Fearless girl' statue dampens spirit behind Wall Street's 'Charging Bull'. 9 Oct. 2017, www.collegiatetimes.com/opinion/fear-less-girl-statue-dampens-spirit-behind-wall-street-s-charging/arti-cle_7ef1e476-ac3f-11e7-a0fe-5bb2dcb8e37e.html (Accessed 12 Oct. 2017).

18. Connelly, T. Fearless Girl statue generates $7.4m in free advertising. 30 Apr. 2017, www.thedrum.com/news/2017/04/30/fearless-girl-stat-ue-generates-74m-free-advertising (Accessed 2 Oct. 2017).

19. Duncan, L. Five secrets of achieving effective ROI from personalised advertising. 10 Jul. 2017, www.thedrum.com/opinion/2017/07/10/five-secrets-achieving-effective-roi-personalised-advertising (Accessed 17 Jul. 2017).

20. Siltanen, R. The Real Story Behind Apple's 'Think Different' Campaign. 14 Dec. 2014, www.forbes.com/sites/onmarketing/2011/12/14/the-re-al-story-behind-apples-think-different-campaign/#162b849b62ab (Accessed 17 Jul. 2017).

21. Haslam, K. Apple ad man speaks about working with Steve Jobs. 21 May 2014, www.macworld.co.uk/feature/apple/apple-ken-segall-think-dif-ferent-jobs-imac-3520866/ (Accessed 18 Jul. 2017).

22. Sunset, B. Think Different Campaign. 3 Mar. 2008, www.market-ing-case-studies.blogspot.be/2008/03/think-different-campaign.html (Accessed 18 Jul. 2017).

23. Sunset, B. (2008).

24. Walsh, F. Salmonella outbreak costs Cadbury £20m. 3 Aug. 2006, www.theguardian.com/business/2006/aug/03/food.foodanddrink (Accessed 18 Jul. 2017).

25. Barreyat-Baron, M. & Barrie, R. Cadbury – How a drumming goril-
    la beat a path back to profitable growth: a real-time effectiveness
    case study. 2008, www.warc.com/SubscriberContent/Article/cad-
    bury_%E2%80%93_how_a_drumming_gorilla_beat_a_path_back_to_
    profitable_growth_a_realtime_effectiveness_case_study/88470 (Ac-
    cessed 18 Jul. 2017).

26. Binet, L. & Field, P. (2017). *Media in focus*. London: Institute of Practi-
    tioners in Advertising.

27. Richards, K. Fearless Girl Stole the World's Heart, but What Did It Do
    for the Client's Business? 10 Sept. 2017, www.adweek.com/brand-mar-
    keting/fearless-girl-stole-the-worlds-heart-but-what-did-it-do-for-the-
    clients-business/(Accessed 21 Sept. 2017).

28. Wikipedia. Standing on the shoulders of giants. 30 May 2017, www.
    en.wikipedia.org/wiki/Standing_on_the_shoulders_of_giants (Ac-
    cessed 18 Jul. 2017).

29. Mostrous, A. YouTube hate preachers share screens with household
    names. 17 Mar. 2017, www.thetimes.co.uk/article/youtube-hate-preach-
    ers-share-screens-with-household-names-kdmpmkkjk (Accessed 21
    Sept. 2017).

30. Slefo, G. Ad Fraud Will Cost $7.2 Billion in 2016, ANA Says, Up Nearly $1
    Billion. 19 Jan. 2016, www.adage.com/article/digital/ana-report-7-2-bil-
    lion-lost-ad-fraud-2015/302201/ (Accessed 21 Sept. 2017).

31. Coldewey, D. Facebook miscalculation significantly inflated aver-
    age video view times for years. 22 Sept. 2016, www.techcrunch.
    com/2016/09/22/facebook-miscalculation-significantly-inflated-aver-
    age-video-view-times-for-years/ (Accessed 21 Sept. 2017).

32. Dua, T. Two of the world's biggest advertisers are cutting back on their
    digital ad spend. 26 Jun. 2017, www.uk.businessinsider.com/two-of-
    the-worlds-biggest-brands-are-cutting-back-on-on-digital-ads-2017-
    6?r=UK&IR=T (Accessed 22 Sept. 2017).

33. Dan, A. With A Single Speech, P&G's Pritchard Signals New Rules
    For Digital Advertising. 4 Mar. 2017, www.forbes.com/sites/av-
    idan/2017/03/04/with-a-single-speech-pgs-pritchard-signals-new-
    rules-for-digital-advertising/#35a5cd0c6176 (Accessed 20 Jul. 2017).

34. Dan, A. P&G's Marc Pritchard On Avoiding The 'Crap Trap' In Advertis-
    ing. 23 Oct. 2016, www.forbes.com/sites/avidan/2016/10/23/pgs-marc-
    pritchard-on-avoiding-the-crap-trap-in-advertising/#eb7050b76f74
    (Accessed 20 Jul. 2017).

35. Smiley, M. P&G's Marc Pritchard says ad landscape needs to 'get simpler'
    and consolidate. 4 Apr. 2017, www.thedrum.com/news/2017/04/04/pg-

s-marc-pritchard-says-ad-landscape-needs-get-simpler-and-consolidate (Accessed 20 Jul. 2017).

36. Bruell, A & Terlep, S. P&G Cuts More Than $100 Million in 'Largely Ineffective' Digital Ads. 27 Jul. 2017, www.wsj.com/articles/p-g-cuts-more-than-100-million-in-largely-ineffective-digital-ads-1501191104 (Accessed 29 Jul. 2017).

37. Staff Writer. '2018 is the year we tackle what's wrong with the industry': Predictions panel & party to highlight what to look for next. 21 Nov. 2017, www.thedrum.com/news/2017/11/21/2018-the-year-we-tackle-what-s-wrong-with-the-industry-predictions-panel-party (Accessed 2 Dec. 2017).

38. Norris, S. How much digital data does an average digital user generate per day and per year? 9 Nov. 2016, www.quora.com/How-much-digital-data-does-an-average-digital-user-generate-per-day-and-per-year (Accessed 20 Jul. 2017).

39. The Economist. Data is giving rise to a new economy. 6 May 2017, www.economist.com/news/briefing/21721634-how-it-shaping-up-data-giving-rise-new-economy (Accessed 20 Jul. 2017).

40. Roderick, L. P&G on how it will deliver personalised messages at scale. 10 Oct. 2017, www.marketingweek.com/2017/10/10/pg-mass-one-one-marketing/ (Accessed 20 Oct. 2017).

41. Talen, A. 6 Evergreen Branding Lessons From Marketing Master David Ogilvy. 21 Feb. 2017, www.talenalexander.com/industry-news/6-evergreen-business-lessons-from-david-ogilvy/ (Accessed 2 Oct. 2017).

42. Warc Staff. TV ads drive 71% of advertising-generated profit. 17 Nov. 2017, www.warc.com/newsandopinion/news/tv_ads_drive_71_of_advertisinggenerated_profit/39612?utm_source=DailyNews&utm_medium=email&utm_campaign=DailyNews20171117 (Accessed 2 Dec. 2017).

43. Schwartz, A.B. The Infamous "War of the Worlds" Radio Broadcast Was a Magnificent Fluke. 6 May 2015, www.smithsonianmag.com/history/infamous-war-worlds-radio-broadcast-was-magnificent-fluke-180955180/ (Accessed 2 Oct. 2017).

44. Chilton, M. The War of the Worlds panic was a myth. 6 May 2016, www.telegraph.co.uk/radio/what-to-listen-to/the-war-of-the-worlds-panic-was-a-myth/ (Accessed 2 Oct. 2017).

45. Govaers, K. & Meacham, M. & Brusselmans, G. Online or traditional advertising, what's better for brands? 16 Nov. 2016, www.bain.com/publications/articles/online-or-traditional-advertising-whats-better-for-brands.aspx (Accessed 10 Oct. 2017).

46. Sullivan, L. Google, Facebook, Microsoft Spent Hundreds Of Millions To Advertise In 2016. 7 Jun. 2017, www.kantarmedia.com/us/newsroom/

km-inthenews/google-facebook-microsoft-spent-hundreds-of-milli-
ons-to-advertise-in-2016 (Accessed 2 Jul. 2017).

47. Goodfellow, J. Online brands now biggest spenders on TV advertising. 23 Feb. 2017, www.thedrum.com/news/2017/02/23/on-
line-brands-now-biggest-spenders-tv-advertising (Accessed 2 Jul. 2017).

48. Captainbijou. 1955 Cadillac Commercial. 8 Apr. 2013, www.youtube.
com/watch?v=1DvhHE7uU30 (Accessed 2 Jul. 2017).

49. Leander, M. 1956 Ford Customline Victoria & Ranch Wagon Car Commercial. 17 Mar. 2011, www.youtube.com/watch?v=a4TLSBolPVc (Accessed 2 Jul. 2017).

50. Leander, M. The famous Snow Plow TV Commercial for Volkswagen
Beetle. 17 Mar. 2011, www.youtube.com/watch?v=VQga04SbTjI (Accessed 2 Jul. 2017).

51. Gianatasio, D. This Short Documentary Tells the Story of the Great
Volkswagen Ads of the '60s. 20 Oct. 2016, www.adweek.com/creativity/
short-documentary-tells-story-great-volkswagen-ads-60s-174168/ (Accessed 12 Jul. 2017).

52. Imseng, D. (2016) *Ugly Is Only Skin-Deep: The Story of the Ads That
Changed the World*. Leicester: Troubador Publishing Ltd.

53. Warc Staff. Pritchard: mass one-to-one marketing is coming. 6 Dec.
2017, www.warc.com/newsandopinion/news/pritchard_mass_one-
toone_marketing_is_coming/39695 (Accessed 10 Dec. 2017).

54. The Metropolitan Museum of Art. Savage Beauty. 6 Dec. 2017, www.
blog.metmuseum.org/alexandermcqueen/about/ (Accessed 10 Dec.
2017).

55. Egil. Pablo Picasso was born in 1881. 25 Oct. 2015, www.carpediem101.
com/october-25-pablo-picasso-was-born-in-1881/ (Accessed 10 Sept.
2017).

56. Loomis, B. 1900-1930: The years of driving dangerously. 26 Apr. 2015,
www.detroitnews.com/story/news/local/michigan-history/2015/04/26/
auto-traffic-history-detroit/26312107/ (Accessed 12 Jul. 2017).

57. Schoelles, L. Social reaction. Dec. 2001, www.schoelles.com/Telephone/
telindex.htm (Accessed 12 Jul. 2017).

58. Stenitzer,, G. What 117 years of content marketing teaches. www.crystal-
clearcomms.com/117-years-content-marketing-teaches-us/ (Accessed 12
Jul. 2017).

59. Wikipedia. Automotive industry in France. 16 Nov. 2017, www.en.wiki-
pedia.org/wiki/Automotive_industry_in_France (Accessed 12 Dec. 2017).

60. Wikipedia. Histoire du téléphone en France. 4 Dec. 2017, www.fr.wikipe-
dia.org/wiki/Histoire_du_t%C3%A9l%C3%A9phone_en_France#En-
tre_1900_et_1950 (Accessed 12 Dec. 2017).

61.	Wikipedia. André Michelin. 4 Dec. 2017, www.en.wikipedia.org/wiki/
	Andr%C3%A9_Michelin (Accessed 12 Dec. 2017).

62.	Michelin. L'Histoire de Michelin. www.michelin.ch/fr/lentreprise/lhis-
	toire (Accessed 4 Dec. 2017).

63.	The Telegraph. Michelin guide 2012: from driver's manual to restaurant
	bible. 4 Nov. 2011, www.telegraph.co.uk/foodanddrink/foodanddrink-
	news/8868836/Michelin-guide-2012-from-drivers-manual-to-restau-
	rant-bible.html (Accessed 2 Jul. 2017).

64.	Jean-François. Guide Michelin edition 1900. 3 Oct. 2016, www.chine-
	et-puces.fr/2016/10/03/guide-michelin-edition-1900/ (Accessed 12 Jul.
	2017).

65.	Park, Y. The History of the Michelin Guide. 31 Oct. 2016, www.guide.
	michelin.co.kr/en/741/history-michelin-guide/ (Accessed 12 Jul. 2017).

66.	Houdoy, E. Les itinéraires Michelin du passé. www.itismich.free.fr/
	index.php (Accessed 23 Jul. 2017).

67.	Fundinguniverse. Dr. August Oetker KG History. www.fundinguniverse.
	com/company-histories/dr-august-oetker-kg-history/ (Accessed 7 Jul.
	2017).

68.	Wikipedia. John Deere. 4 Dec. 2017, www.en.wikipedia.org/wiki/John_
	Deere_(inventor) (Accessed 12 Dec. 2017).

69.	John Deere. Past leaders. www.deere.com/en/our-company/about-john-
	deere/past-leaders/john-deere/ (Accessed 4 Jul. 2017).

70.	Lazauskas, J. This Is What Content Marketing Looked Like in the 1800s.
	6 Jan. 2017, www.contently.com/strategist/2017/01/06/the-furrow-
	1800s-content/ (Accessed 4 Jul. 2017).

71.	Bauer, E. A Brief History Of Content Marketing (It's Not As New As You
	Think). 20 May 2014, www.hub.uberflip.com/blog/a-brief-history-of-
	content-marketing (Accessed 4 Jul. 2017).

72.	John Deere. About us. www.deere.com/en/our-company/about-john-
	deere/ (Accessed 4 Jul. 2017).

73.	Mathews, J.P. & Schultz G.P. (2009). *Chicle: The Chewing Gum of the Amer-
	icas, from the Ancient Maya to William Wrigley*. Tuscon: The University of
	Arizona Press.

74.	Mathews, J.P. & Schultz G.P. (2009).

75.	Weiser, K. Legendary Route 66. Where are the Burma Shave signs?. Mar.
	2017, www.legendsofamerica.com/66-burmashave.html (Accessed 4 Jul.
	2017).

76.	Adage. Burma Shave. 15 Sept. 2014, www.adage.com/article/adage-en-
	cyclopedia/burma-shave/98367/ (Accessed 22 Jul. 2017).

77.	Coombs, D. & Batchelor, B. (2014). *We are what we sell. How advertising
	shapes American life*. Santa Barbara: Praeger.

78. Schutz. Burma Shave Slogans. www.skypoint.com/members/schutz19/burma2.htm (Accessed 11 Sept. 2017).

79. Wikipedia. Halo Effect. 1 Dec. 2017, www.en.wikipedia.org/wiki/Halo_effect#CITEREFThorndike1920 (Accessed 12 Dec. 2017).

80. Sickels, R. (2013). *100 Entertainers Who Changed America: An Encyclopedia of Pop Culture Luminaries*. Santa Barbara: Greenwood.

81. Williams, P. & Williams, R. (2008). *How to Be Like Women of Power: Wisdom and Advice to Create Your Own Destiny*. Deerfield Beach: Health Communications, Inc.

82. Williams, P. & Williams, R. (2008).

83. Watson, J.T. Johnny Roventini: Unique *and* Euphonious! 2005, www.lucyfan.com/johnnyroventini.html (Accessed 8 Jul. 2017).

84. Wikipedia. Johnny Roventini. 16 Oct. 2017, www.en.wikipedia.org/wiki/Johnny_Roventini (Accessed 12 Dec. 2017).

85. Wikipedia. Philip Morris Playhouse. 25 Jun. 2017, www.en.wikipedia.org/wiki/Philip_Morris_Playhouse (Accessed 12 Dec. 2017).

86. Grant, M. A'I Love Lucy: Ultimate Season One' Is Really Smokin'. 8 May 2014, www.popmatters.com/181564-i-love-lucy-ultimate-season-one-2495663016.html (Accessed 13 Jul. 2017).

87. Samuel, L.R. (2001). *Brought to You By: Postwar Television Advertising and the American Dream*. Austin: University of Texas Press

88. As P&G's Soap Opera Era Ends, Our Innovation in Entertainment Continues. 13 Sept. 2010, www.news.pg.com/blog/entertainment/pgs-soap-opera-era-ends-our-innovation-entertainment-continues#st-hash.WHAf9VPY.dpuf (Accessed 1 Dec. 2017).

89. Shmoop Editorial Team. Economy in the 1950s. 11 Nov. 2011, www.shmoop.com/1950s/economy.html (Accessed 2 Aug. 2017).

90. Usher, S. Let us blaze new trails. 24 Jun. 2013, www.lettersofnote.com/2013/06/let-us-blaze-new-trails.html (Accessed 4 Aug. 2017).

91. Roman, K. (2009). *The King of Madison Avenue: David Ogilvy and the Making of Modern Advertising*. New York: Palgrave Macmillan.

92. Stevenson, S. 'We try harder': The story of most brilliant ad slogan of the 20th century. 12 Aug 2016, www.mercurynews.com/2013/08/13/we-try-harder-the-story-of-most-brilliant-ad-slogan-of-the-20th-century/ (Accessed 14 Aug. 2017).

93. Makovsky, K. A 'Big Idea' That Delivered. 21 Feb. 2013, www.forbes.com/sites/kenmakovsky/2013/02/21/a-big-idea-that-delivered/#285862e5726b (Accessed 14 Aug. 2017).

94. Stevenson, S. (2016).

95. Stevenson, S. We're No. 2! We're No. 2! 12 Aug. 2013, www.slate.com/articles/business/rivalries/2013/08/hertz_vs_avis_advertising_wars_

how_an_ad_firm_made_a_virtue_out_of_second.html (Accessed 14 Aug. 2017).

96. Stevenson, S. (2016).

97. Stevenson, S. (2013).

98. Elliott, S. The Media Business: Advertising; Leo Burnett is named one of the business leaders of the century. 27 Nov. 1998, www.nytimes.com/1998/11/27/business/media-business-advertising-leo-burnett-named-one-business-leaders-century.html (Accessed 14 Aug. 2017).

99. Upfront Analytics. System 1 vs System 2 Decision Making. 2015, www.upfrontanalytics.com/market-research-system-1-vs-system-2-decision-making/ (Accessed 14 Aug. 2017).

100. Kahneman, D. (2011). *Thinking fast and slow*. New York: Farrar, Straus and Giroux.

101. Shotton, R. Fast and slow lessons for marketers. 7 Apr. 2014, www.theguardian.com/media-network/media-network-blog/2014/apr/07/thinking-fast-slow-marketers-consumers (Accessed 11 Aug. 2017).

102. De Meulemeester, P. System 1 Autopilot Fast Implicit. 14 Jan. 2015, www.slideshare.net/philipdemeulemeester/behavioural-economics-in/32-System_1AutopilotFastImplicitEffortlessAssociativeDifficult_to_control_or (Accessed 11 Aug. 2017).

103. Vranica, S. Average Tenure of CMO Continues To Decline. 17 Mar. 2017, www.wsj.com/articles/average-tenure-of-cmo-continues-to-decline-1489777765?mg=prod/accounts-wsj (Accessed 11 Aug. 2017).

104. Dan, A. (2017).

105. Kay, G. Marketing is stuck in first gear. 31 Oct. 2017, www.warc.com/newsandopinion/opinion/marketing_is_stuck_in_first_gear/2549?utm_source=DailyNews&utm_medium=email&utm_campaign=DailyNews20171102 (Accessed 23 Nov. 2017).

106. Dentsu Aegis Network, own research.

107. Ritson, M. Spreadsheet jockeys are misunderstanding the marketing funnel. 20 Sept. 2017, www.marketingweek.com/2017/09/20/mark-ritson-collapse-marketing-funnel/ (Accessed 12 Nov. 2017).

108. Littunen, M. & Evans, J. & McCabe, D. & Worsley, G. Mounting risks to marketing effectiveness. 18 May 2017, www.darkroom.magnetic.media/original/7352eda4b775a9ba544a45b390502c1e:5eea43f65bb4b-c8c79a12266f5f8ee76/magnetic-enders-report-mounting-risks-to-marketing-effectiveness-exective-summary.pdf (Accessed 12 Jul. 2017).

109. Binet, L. & Field, P. (2017).

110. Binet, L. & Field, P. (2017).

111. Binet, L. & Field, P. (2017).

112. Gomez-Uribe, C & Hunt, N. (2016) The Netflix Recommender System: Algorithms, Business Value, and Innovation. *ACM Transactions on Management Information Systems, 6 (4), 13.*

113. Titcomb, J. Google hit with record £2.1bn EU fine for abusing internet search monopoly. 27 Jun. 2017, www.telegraph.co.uk/technology/2017/06/27/eu-hits-google-record-21bn-fine-abusing-internet-search-monopoly/ (Accessed 12 Jul. 2017).

114. Bloom, A. How the Web Affects Memory. Nov.-Dec. 2011, www.harvardmagazine.com/2011/11/how-the-web-affects-memory (Accessed 14 Jul. 2017).

115. Kinsella, B. 42 Percent of US Smartphone Owners Use AI Personal Assistant Monthly. 28 Jul. 2017, www.voicebot.ai/2017/07/28/42-percent-us-smartphone-owners-use-ai-personal-assistant-monthly/ (Accessed 29 Jul. 2017).

116. Warc Staff. Amazon Echo set to hit 40% of UK homes by next year. 11 May 2017, www.warc.com/NewsAndOpinion/News/Amazon_Echo_set_to_hit_40_of_UK_homes_by_next_year/38648 (Accessed 2 Oct. 2017).

117. Dunn, J. Here's how Amazon Echo owners actually use their smart speakers. 4 Oct. 2016, www.uk.businessinsider.com/amazon-echo-most-used-features-2016-10?international=true&r=UK&IR=T (Accessed 2 Oct. 2017).

118. L2 Gartner. Amazon Intelligence: Voice. 5 Jul. 2017, www.l2inc.com/research/voice (Accessed 2 Oct. 2017).

119. BI Intelligence. Amazon Echo owners are spending more money on Amazon. 20 Sept. 2016, www.uk.businessinsider.com/amazon-echo-owners-are-spending-more-money-on-amazon-2016-9?utm_source=feedly&utm_medium=webfeeds&r=US&IR=T (Accessed 2 Oct. 2017).

120. Smith, G. 12 amazing Amazon Alexa statistics and facts. 26 Nov. 2017, www.expandedramblings.com/index.php/amazon-alexa-statistics/#.Wdd69caB3UI (Accessed 2 Dec. 2017).

121. Young, V.M. Amazon's Alexa Could Change How Consumers Shop for Brands — Or Not. 26 Nov. 2017, www.wwd.com/business-news/business-features/amazons-alexa-could-mean-some-brands-wont-matter-voice-experience-online-outlet-10867063/ (Accessed 2 Dec. 2017).

122. Hempel, J. Voice Is the Next Big Platform, and Alexa Will Own it. 19 Dec. 2016, www.wired.com/2016/12/voice-is-the-next-big-platform-and-alexa-will-own-it/ (Accessed 2 Aug. 2017).

123. Swant, M. The voice assistant is growing much faster than Google's version. 7 Jul. 2017, www.adweek.com/digital/alexa-is-more-likely-to-recommend-amazon-prime-products-according-to-new-research/ (Accessed 2 Aug. 2017).

124. L2 Gartner. Amazon Intelligence: Voice. 5 Jul. 2017, www.l2inc.com/re-search/voice (Accessed 2 Oct. 2017).

125. eMarketer. Alexa, Say What?! Voice-Enabled Speaker Usage to Grow Nearly 130% This Year. 8 May 2017, www.emarketer.com/Article/Alexa-Say-What-Voice-Enabled-Speaker-Usage-Grow-Nearly-130-This-Year/1015812 (Accessed 2 Oct. 2017).

126. McGrath, F. 1 in 3 Gen Z in North America Using Voice Command on Mobile. 22 Sept. 2017, www.blog.globalwebindex.net/chart-of-the-day/1-in-3-gen-z-north-america-using-voice-command-on-mobile/ (Accessed 5 Aug. 2017).

127. Fernandez, A. Engaging Gen Z. www.ketchum.com/engaging-gen-z (Accessed 1 Oct. 2017).

128. Skyler, H. Show Me, Says Gen Z: Pivotals Want Proof. www.millennial-marketing.com/2017/01/show-me-says-gen-z-pivotals-want-proof/ (Accessed 1 Oct. 2017).

129. Statista. Top ice cream brands of the United States in 2017, based on sales (in million U.S. dollars). www.statista.com/statistics/190426/top-ice-cream-brands-in-the-united-states/ (Accessed 1 Oct. 2017).

130. Carissimo, J. Ben & Jerry's publicly endorses Black Lives Matter. 7 Oct. 2016, www.independent.co.uk/news/world/americas/ben-jerry-s-ex-plains-why-black-lives-matter-a7351321.html (Accessed 5 Jul. 2017).

131. Warc Staff. Axe Styling: Not Just A Pretty Hairstyle. 2017, www.warc.com/SubscriberContent/Article/axe_styling_not_just_a_pretty_hair-style/111451 (Accessed 5 Jul. 2017).

132. Fromm, J. How Unilever Is Winning With Millennials And Gen Z. 31 Jan. 2017, www.forbes.com/sites/jefffromm/2017/01/31/how-unilever-is-winning-with-millennials-and-gen-z/#743427b552fd (Accessed 5 Jul. 2017).

133. Bauwens, D. & Evers, F. Millennials willen de wereld verbeteren, zolang het geen pijn doet. 29 Aug. 2017, www.demorgen.be/economie/millen-nials-willen-de-wereld-verbeteren-zolang-het-geen-pijn-doet-ba718d46/ (Accessed 5 Sept. 2017).

134. Fromm, J. (2017).

135. VANTYGHEM, P. Slaap tiener, slaap. 5 Sept. 2017, www.standaard.be/cnt/dmf20170904_03053697 (Accessed 3 Oct. 2017).

136. Patel, D. 10 Tips For Marketing To Gen Z Consumers. 1 May 2017, www.forbes.com/sites/deeppatel/2017/05/01/10-tips-for-market-ing-to-gen-z-consumers/#2eb157eb3c50 (Accessed 3 Oct. 2017).

137. Maybin, S. Busting the attention span myth. 10 Mar. 2017, www.bbc.com/news/health-38896790 (Accessed 3 Oct. 2017).

138. Finch, J. What Is Generation Z, And What Does It Want? 5 Apr. 2015, www.fastcompany.com/3045317/what-is-generation-z-and-what-does-it-want (Accessed 3 Oct. 2017).

139. Kantar Millward Brown. AdReaction: Engaging Gen X, Y and Z. 10 Jan. 2017, www.millwardbrown.com/adreaction/genxyz/uk/home (Accessed 3 Oct. 2017).

140. Sterling, G. Study: Gen Z more discriminating, more advertising-resistant than Gen X or Y. 11 Jan. 2017, www.marketingland.com/study-gen-z-discriminating-advertising-resistant-gen-x-y-203007 (Accessed 16 Jul. 2017).

141. Stengel, J. Study: 2017 ANA Masters of Marketing – Day 2. 6 Oct. 2017, www.marketingland.com/study-gen-z-discriminating-advertising-resistant-gen-x-y-203007 (Accessed 16 Oct. 2017).

142. The Guardian. Study: Maya Angelou quotes: 15 of the best. 29 May 2014, www.theguardian.com/books/2014/may/28/maya-angelou-in-fifteen-quotes (Accessed 16 Oct. 2017).

143. Brandt, D. Study: Emotions Give a Lift to Advertising. 2016, www.nielsen.com/content/dam/nielsenglobal/us/docs/solutions/emotions-give-a-lift-to-advertising.pdf (Accessed 16 Oct. 2017).

144. Wikipedia. Johnnie Walker. 25 Jun. 2017, www.en.wikipedia.org/wiki/Johnnie_Walker (Accessed 12 Dec. 2017).

145. Wikipedia. Roberto Baggio. 25 Jun. 2017, www.en.wikipedia.org/wiki/Roberto_Baggio (Accessed 2 Jul. 2017).

146. Fairbanks, M. Hello Man on the Moon and hello again to the 'John Lewis' effect. 6 Nov. 2015, www.campaignlive.co.uk/article/hello-man-moon-hello-again-john-lewis-effect/1371678 (Accessed 17 Oct. 2017).

147. Harrington, J. John Lewis christmas campaign gets 22.429 tweets in one hour as #manonthemoon gets UK talking (Online). 6 Nov. 2015, www.prweek.com/article/1371645/john-lewis-christmas-campaign-gets-22429-tweets-one-hour-manonthemoon-gets-uk-talking (Accessed 18 Oct. 2017).

148. Charron, C. John Lewis' 'Man on the Moon' Campaign in Numbers & Learnings. 9 Nov. 2015, www.blog.360i.com/social-marketing/john-lewis-man-on-the-moon-campaign-in-numbers-learnings (Accessed 18 Oct. 2017).

149. Ideal Home. The best #ManOnTheMoon goodies from the John Lewis Christmas campaign. 6 Nov. 2015, www.idealhome.co.uk/news/john-lewis-christmas-man-on-the-moon-merchandise-18343 (Accessed 18 Oct. 2017).

150. Hobbs, T. John Lewis sees a significant sales uplift following 'Man on the Moon' launch. 20 Nov. 2015, www.marketingweek.com/2015/11/20/

john-lewis-sees-a-significant-sales-uplift-following-man-on-the-moon-launch/ (Accessed 20 Oct. 2017).

151. Binet, L. & Field, P. (2013). *The Long and the Short of It*. London: Institute of Practitioners in Advertising.

152. Binet, L. & Field, P. (2013).

153. Ellis, G.E. & Smith, M. & Berry, A. & Gladdis, S. & Wragg, M. T-Mobile - Life's for sharing, even in a recession. 2010, www.warc.com/SubscriberContent/Article/tmobile__lifes_for_sharing,_even_in_a_recession/92509 (Accessed 20 Oct. 2017).

154. Lockhaart. T-Mobile Case Study. 6 May 2011, www.adpitch.wordpress.com/2011/05/06/t-mobile-dance-flash-mob-case-study/ (Accessed 1 Oct. 2017).

155. UTalkMarketing. T-Mobile 'Dance' Integrated campaign. 3 Aug. 2009, www.utalkmarketing.com/pages/article.aspx?articleid=14797&title=t-mobile_da (Accessed 1 Oct. 2017).

156. Idem.

157. Warc Staff. Spies Travels: Do it for Denmark, Mom and Spies. 2017, www.warc.com/SubscriberContent/Article/spies_travels_do_it_for_denmark,_mom_and_spies/111650 (Accessed 1 Oct. 2017).

158. ABMA/BVAM. Tell a Vision 2017 | Les Binet. 5 Oct. 2017, www.youtube.com/watch?time_continue=685&v=xhfMlc6CPgA (Accessed 6 Oct. 2017).

159. Günbal, B. The Psychology of Sharing: why do people share online? 11 Sept. 2011, www.slideshare.net/gunbal/the-psychology-of-sharing-why-do-people-share-online (Accessed 2 Jul. 2017).

160. Libert, K. & Tynski, K. The emotions that make marketing campaigns go viral. 24 Oct 2013, www.hbr.org/2013/10/research-the-emotions-that-make-marketing-campaigns-go-viral (Accessed 2 Feb. 2017).

161. Ekman, P. (2003). *Emotions Revealed*. New York: Times Books.

162. Tynski, K. Here's how to go viral: use the emotions of highly viral content. 9 Jul. 2013, www.frac.tl/viral-emotions-study/ (Accessed 2 Feb. 2017).

163. Opensource. What is open source?. www.opensource.com/resources/what-open-source (Accessed 6 Oct. 2017).

164. Ogunyemi, L. I am the woman in the 'racist Dove ad'. I am not a victim. 10 Oct. 2017, www.theguardian.com/commentisfree/2017/oct/10/i-am-woman-racist-dove-ad-not-a-victim (Accessed 19 Oct. 2017).

165. Johnson, O. How Dove changed the rules of the beauty game. 2005, www.warc.com/SubscriberContent/Article/how_dove_changed_the_rules_of_the_beauty_game/81127 (Accessed 19 Oct. 2017).

166. Johnson, O. (2005).

167. Warc Staff. Dove "the campaign for real beauty". 2007, www.warc.com/SubscriberContent/Article/dove_'the_campaign_for_real_beauty'/89583 (Accessed 1 Oct. 2017).

168. Schultz, E.J. After Kendall Jenner Ad Debacle, What's Next For Pepsi? 6 Apr. 2017, www.adage.com/article/cmo-strategy/kendall-jenner-ad-debacle-pepsi/308587/ (Accessed 1 Oct. 2017).

169. Schultz, E.J. Pepsi's Kendall Jenner joins a protest AD sparks backlash. 4 Apr. 2017, www.adage.com/article/cmo-strategy/pepsi-s-kendall-jenner-ad-sparks-backlash/308563/ (Accessed 2 Oct. 2017).

170. Idem.

171. Whiteside, S. Unilever steps up from marketing purpose to brand activism. Sept. 2017, www.warc.com/SubscriberContent/Article/A108732_Unilever_steps_up_from_marketing_purpose_to_brand_activism/108732 (Accessed 4 Oct. 2017).

172. Idem.

173. Warc Staff. Media Markt: Rabbit Race AME Awards. 2016, www.warc.com/SubscriberContent/Article/media_markt_rabbit_race/106759 (Accessed 4 Oct. 2017).

174. Warc Staff. Media Markt: Rabbit Race Cannes Creative Lions. 2016, www.warc.com/SubscriberContent/Article/media_markt_rabbit_race/107644 (Accessed 4 Oct. 2017).

175. Warc Staff. John Lewis: Monty's Christmas Cannes Creative Lions. 2016, www.warc.com/SubscriberContent/Article/john_lewis_montys_christmas/107637 (Accessed 10 Oct. 2017).

176. Coscia, A. Always #LikeaGirl: Changing the meaning of words to make girls proud to be girls. 2015, www.warc.com/SubscriberContent/Article/always_likeagirl_changing_the_meaning_of_words_to_make_girls_proud_to_be_girls/105159 (Accessed 10 Oct. 2017).

177. Moore, C. Obama: girls power's 'badass'. 28 Oct. 2015, www.nydailynews.com/sports/soccer/obama-girls-power-badass-article-1.2414842 (Accessed 15 Oct. 2017).

178. Precourt, G. P&G's #likeagirl continues to dazzle. Feb. 2015, www.warc.com/SubscriberContent/Article/pamp;gs_likeagirl_continues_to_dazzle/106859 (Accessed 15 Jul. 2017).

179. Ward, M. McDonald's pulls 'exploitative' UK ad featuring boy trying to connect with deceased dad. 17 May 2017, www.mumbrella.com.au/mcdonalds-pulls-exploitative-uk-ad-featuring-boy-trying-connect-deceased-dad-445247 (Accessed 15 Jul. 2017).

180. Delgado, D. Here's Why That Heineken Ad Is Even Worse Than The Pepsi Ad. 2 May 2017, www.huffingtonpost.com/entry/the-heineken-

ad-is-worse-than-the-pepsi-ad-youre_us_5903decee4b05279d4edbc1f (Accessed 15 Jul. 2017).

181. Pantagonia. Don't Buy This Jacket, Black Friday and the New York Times. 17 May 2017, www.patagonia.com/blog/2011/11/dont-buy-this-jacket-black-friday-and-the-new-york-times/ (Accessed 15 Jul. 2017).

182. Warc Staff. Patagonia takes on Trump. 6 Dec. 2017, www.warc.com/newsandopinion/news/patagonia_takes_on_trump/39710?utm_source=DailyNews&utm_medium=email&utm_campaign=Daily-News20171206 (Accessed 20 Dec. 2017).

183. Ben & Jerry's. Imagine This Pint Is Our Democracy. 27 Jul. 2016, www.youtube.com/watch?v=vNzXxYnQI3s (Accessed 15 Jul. 2017).

184. Simms, E. Volvo Case Study. 11 Oct. 2016, www.prezi.com/ltx4qr_0s9x0/volvo-case-study/ (Accessed 16 Dec. 2017).